insight text guide

Anja Drummond

The Boy in the Striped Pyjamas

John Boyne

First published in 2021, reprinted in 2023, 2025, 2026.

Insight Publications Pty Ltd
3/350 Charman Road
Cheltenham VIC 3192
Australia
Tel: +61 3 8571 4950
Email: books@insightpublications.com.au

www.insightpublications.com.au

A catalogue record for this book is available from the National Library of Australia

John Boyne's The Boy in the Striped Pyjamas / Anja Drummond

Anja Drummond asserts the moral right to be identified as the author of this work.

ISBNs:
9781922525468 (print)
9781922525475 (digital)

Cover design by Gisela Beer

Proudly Printed in Australia by Ligare Book Printers

contents

CHARACTER MAP

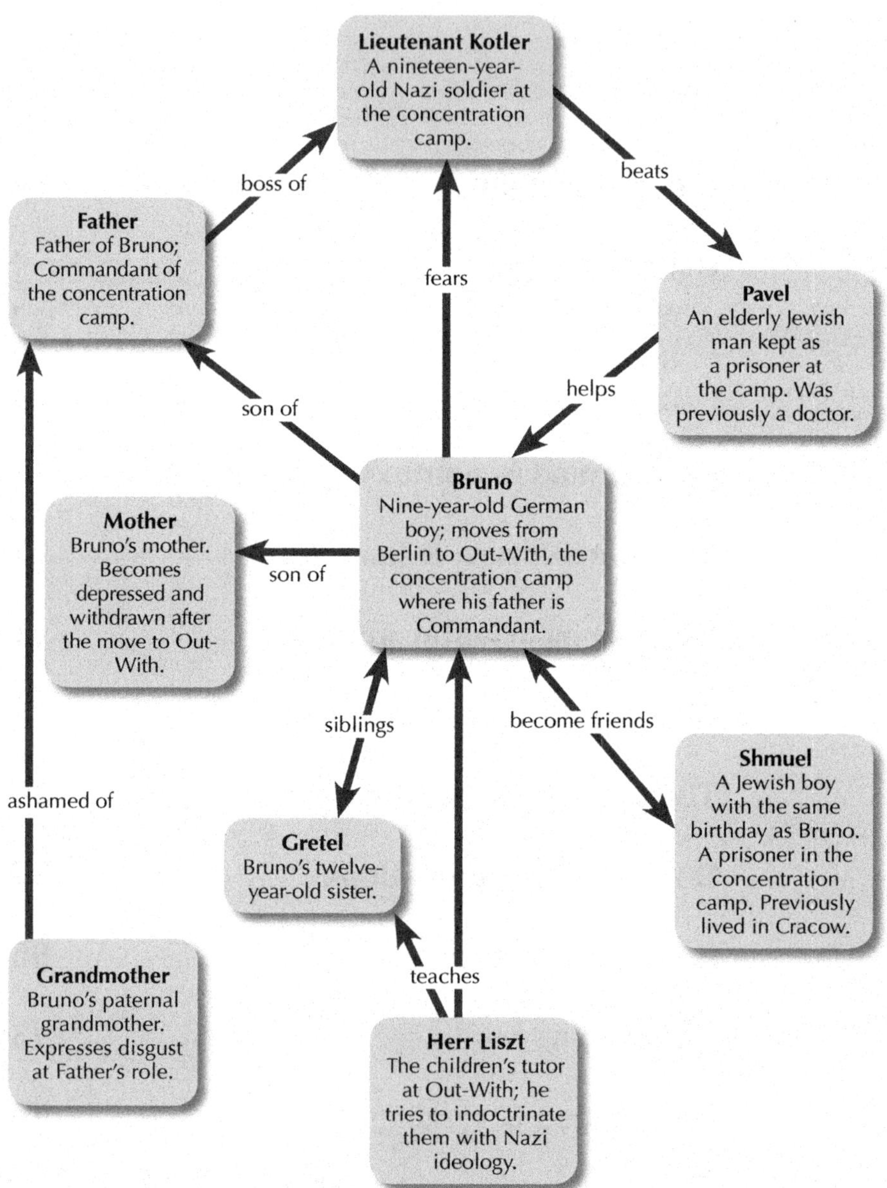

OVERVIEW

About the author

Born in Dublin, Ireland on 30 April 1971, John Boyne is a prolific and acclaimed author of fiction for both children and adults.

From a young age, Boyne was an avid reader, devouring literary classics such as *The Count of Monte Cristo, Robinson Crusoe* and *Treasure Island*. This love of literature evolved into a passion for writing, a love that Boyne pursued in his tertiary education. However, his childhood was also marred by the horror of sexual abuse at the hands of priests and teachers, something that he opened up about in 2014 in an article in *The Irish Times* (Boyne 2014). In addition, Boyne was forced to struggle with the challenge of being a gay teenager in a community where 'the importance of church life ... cannot be overstated' and where homosexuality remained criminalised until Boyne was in his third year of university. While he spent many years seeking to push aside this part of his life, Boyne drew upon aspects of this experience for his 2014 novel *A History of Loneliness,* hoping that this novel might help 'those who blindly defend the church against all critics [to] recognise the crimes that the institution has committed, while those who condemn it ceaselessly might accept that there are many decent people who have lived good lives within it' (Boyne 2014).

Boyne completed a Bachelor of Arts (English Literature) at Trinity College Dublin and a Master of Arts (Creative Writing) at the University of East Anglia, and in 2015 he was awarded an honorary Doctorate of Letters by the University of East Anglia. Throughout his career, Boyne has received numerous literary awards, including the Hennessy Literary 'Hall of Fame' Award for his body of work. For his 2006 novel *The Boy in the Striped Pyjamas* alone he received the Irish Book Awards Children's Book of the Year (Senior), Irish Book Awards Listener's Choice Book of the Year, Bisto Book of the Year, Que Leer Award Best International Novel of the

Year (Spain), and the Orange Prize Readers Group Book of the Year. It is a testament to the strength of Boyne's writing that his works have been translated into fifty-four languages, including Dutch, Russian, Spanish, Danish, Hungarian, Slovenian and Portuguese.

Although not intentional, in his efforts to write stories that are meaningful and relevant to the modern reader Boyne has courted controversy. *The Boy in the Striped Pyjamas*, though lauded by many as a powerful story that evokes the horrors of the Holocaust, is viewed by some reviewers very negatively (see 'Different interpretations' for more on this). More recently, Boyne was at the centre of an online furore regarding his young adult novel *My Brother's Name is Jessica*, in which a young person's gender transition is seen through the eyes of their brother.

Synopsis

Note: While it is accepted that 'Out-With' is intended to be Bruno's childish mispronunciation of Auschwitz, the camp is referred to as Out-With throughout this guide in recognition that Boyne's novel is a fictional interpretation that contains historical inaccuracies.

Nine-year-old Bruno arrives home to find the family's maid, Maria, packing his belongings. Bruno is stunned to learn his family are moving far away from Berlin. He is told his father has been given a new job by 'the Fury' (the Führer, Adolf Hitler). Through flashbacks, it becomes apparent that Father was specially singled out by Hitler for the role of Commandant (officer in charge) of 'Out-With' (Bruno's mispronunciation of Auschwitz). It also emerges that Bruno's grandmother is unhappy with her son's role.

Bruno immediately dislikes his new home at Out-With – it is cold and isolated. Many soldiers come in and out of Father's office every day, but it is 'Out Of Bounds' for Bruno. From Bruno's bedroom window he can see a huge wire fence that is 'not fifty feet away from their new home' (p.37) and there are people (including children) on the other side who 'looked as if they were crying' (p.38). On Bruno's side of the fence the only other child is his twelve-year-old sister Gretel, whom he does not get along with at all.

Bruno seeks ways to keep himself busy within the confines of the property; for example, he tries to make a tyre swing but falls off and injures himself. With no other adult around to care for Bruno, Pavel (who Bruno has seen working in the house doing domestic chores such as peeling potatoes) comes to his aid. Pavel tends to Bruno's wounds, revealing that he is a doctor, which confuses Bruno.

Bruno's explorations move beyond the home, despite the fact that this is forbidden. He comes across a Jewish boy, Shmuel, sitting on the other side of the fence, who wears the 'striped pyjamas' that the people Bruno has seen through his window also wear. The boys begin to talk, discovering that they share the same birthday, and a friendship quickly develops. Shmuel tells Bruno stories of his life before he came to Out-With, and of life at the camp, yet Bruno struggles to comprehend what his new friend is talking about.

After some months, Bruno receives a shock when he finds Shmuel cleaning in his home. Having noted that his friend is even thinner than he was before, Bruno feeds Shmuel some leftover chicken, but Lieutenant Kotler (a young soldier whom Bruno dislikes) becomes angry when he discovers Shmuel has eaten. Bruno fails to defend Shmuel, who is beaten, and Bruno is filled with shame. On another occasion Bruno witnesses Kotler's brutality when he beats Pavel for spilling wine when serving the family. Although Bruno receives lessons from a tutor named Herr Liszt that are designed to inculcate in him the Nazi ideology, he continues to feel a great sense of connection to Shmuel.

More than a year passes. Mother convinces Father that she and the children should return to Berlin. Bruno unhappily reveals this news to Shmuel, while Shmuel reveals that his father has gone missing. The boys plan an adventure: Bruno is to dress up in the pyjamas worn on the other side of the fence, crawl under the fence and help Shmuel find his father. As they search, the boys are caught up in a march and pushed forward by soldiers into a dry, airtight room (they do not realise it is a gas chamber). Scared, the boys hold hands as darkness engulfs them. This is the last time Bruno is heard from. After some time in which searches for Bruno are fruitless, his mother and sister return to Berlin while Father remains. Father eventually discovers the pile of clothes Bruno left at the fence line and pieces together what must have happened to his son. The novel concludes with the arrival of different soldiers (the Allies), to whom Father submits, no longer caring what happens to him.

Character summaries

Bruno

The nine-year-old protagonist. Bruno loves to explore and enjoys adventure stories. He is intimidated by his father's assertive and authoritative personality and he usually follows his parents' strict rules. Bruno is ignorant of the complexity of the world around him and tends to be self-centred. When he is surprised by something, his 'mouth [makes] the shape of an O' (p.7).

Father

Bruno's father – his name is Ralf (p.94). From what he has overheard, Bruno understands that Father is 'a man to watch and … the Fury had big things in mind for him' (p.4). Father believes in German superiority and considers what he does as Commandant to be important work, believing that Jewish people are 'not people at all' (p.55).

Grandmother

The mother of Bruno's father. A singer in her youth, Grandmother (Nathalie, p.94) loves to perform and Bruno has fond memories of her. Grandmother disagrees with the actions and policies of the Nazi party and despises Father's work. Grandmother dies while the family live at Out-With.

Grandfather

The father of Bruno's father. He is proud of his son's advancement in the Nazi party, believing that he is helping Germany 'reclaim her pride after all the great wrongs that were done to her' (p.95).

Gretel

Bruno's twelve-year-old sister, referred to by Bruno as a 'Hopeless Case' (p.3). Gretel considers herself far more mature than her younger brother. She is initially almost as ignorant as her brother but her lessons with Herr Liszt indoctrinate her. Gretel has a crush on Lieutenant Kotler.

Herr Liszt

Bruno and Gretel's tutor when they live at Out-With. Herr Liszt teaches the children history and geography in an effort to indoctrinate them.

Karl, Daniel, and Martin

Bruno's 'three best friends for life' (p.8) from Berlin. By the end of the novel Bruno struggles to remember them.

Lars

The family's butler in Berlin who comes with them to Out-With.

Lieutenant Kotler

A cruel and violent nineteen-year-old Nazi lieutenant whose 'yellow-blond hair' (p.73) meets the Aryan ideal. Bruno dislikes (and even fears) Kotler, who refers to Bruno as 'little man' (p.74). After it is revealed that his father fled Germany in 1938, Kotler is transferred away from Out-With.

Maria

The family's long-serving maid who comes to Out-With with them. Although Maria inwardly disagrees with Father's work, she is grateful for what he has done for her and her mother in the past.

Mother

Bruno's mother. Mother becomes increasingly withdrawn and often drinks 'medicinal sherries' (p.194) to cope with her depression from living at Out-With. It is implied that she spends too much time with Kotler and perhaps flirts with him. Mother tends to speak to her son in vague generalisations.

Pavel

An elderly Jewish prisoner who worked as a doctor before the Nazis invaded Poland. He is forced to come to the family home each day to 'help peel the vegetables ... before putting his white jacket on and serving at the table' (p.77).

Shmuel

A Jewish prisoner at Out-With, Shmuel shares a birthday with Bruno. He is the titular 'boy in the striped pyjamas'. Unlike Bruno, Shmuel is painfully aware of the horrors of the camp, where starvation, fear and violence are part of his day-to-day experience. Over the course of his friendship with Bruno, Shmuel becomes thinner and weaker every day, and his grandfather and father disappear. Shmuel is a character foil for Bruno.

The Fury

Adolf Hitler, who was referred to as the Führer (a German word that means leader). Bruno meets him briefly when the Fury comes to the family's home in Berlin for dinner. Bruno does not like him, finding him rude.

BACKGROUND & CONTEXT

In order to comprehend the nuances of Boyne's novel, a clear understanding of the nature of Nazi ideology and the actions undertaken by Germany during the Holocaust, especially at Auschwitz, is needed. It is also important to recognise that there are deliberate historical inaccuracies in Boyne's narrative.

The Treaty of Versailles

When World War I ended on 11 November 1918, Germany experienced significant political upheaval. This upheaval was a consequence of the overthrow of Germany's monarchy and its replacement by a democratic government known as the Weimar Republic. It was also a consequence of the harsh terms imposed upon Germany in the Treaty of Versailles, signed in 1919. These terms included the surrender of vast amounts of land, demilitarisation, and the 'War Guilt clause' that forced Germany to accept full responsibility for starting the war and pay reparations (the equivalent of $33 billion) to the Allied powers. Germany had no hope of paying these reparations in full. In fact, it was predicted by economists that the European economy would collapse from the financial burden, a prediction that proved to be accurate.

The rise of the Nazi Party

Founded in 1920, the National Socialist Workers' Party, or Nazi Party, was a radical far-right movement led by Adolf Hitler. The ideology of the Nazis was racist and nationalist in nature, with anti-Semitism (prejudice against or hatred of Jewish people) forming a clear cornerstone of their policies. It was their belief that a strong German state was needed to lead the 'master race' against 'inferior races' such as the Romani (an Indo-Aryan ethnic group) and Jewish people.

Hitler realised that, to destroy the Weimar Republic, the Nazi Party initially needed to achieve political power within the nation's democratic processes. At first, the German electorate gave little support to the Nazi Party. However, the sufferings brought about by the Great Depression – economic unrest, poverty and unemployment – provided an opportunity for the Nazis to increase support as the people lost faith in the ability of the Weimar Republic to address these issues. This is demonstrated by their success in winning 18.3 per cent of votes in the 1930 Reichstag (lower chamber of parliament) elections, and 37.4 per cent of votes in the 1932 elections. As a result of political manoeuvring, on 30 January 1933 Hitler was appointed chancellor of a coalition government.

Once Hitler became chancellor, he moved swiftly to manipulate the political situation to create an authoritarian state. Following the Reichstag (parliament building) fire on 27 February 1933, Hitler declared a state of emergency, abolishing civil liberties and centralising control. Soon after, through arrests and intimidation, he passed the Enabling Act. This allowed him to create laws without the approval of the Reichstag or the President. Then, on 14 July 1933, all other political parties were abolished, making Germany a one-party state under Nazi rule. Following the death of President Hindenburg in August 1934, Hitler declared himself Führer, thereby becoming the absolute ruler of Germany.

Having consolidated political power, Hitler and his party were able to pursue their agenda. The Nuremberg Race Laws, passed on 15 September 1935, defined Jewish people as members of a race rather than holders of particular religious beliefs. Specifically, the laws legalised the persecution of Jews, excluded them from Reich citizenship, and prohibited them from marrying or having sexual relations with persons of non-Jewish German blood. These laws also denied German Jews the right to vote or hold public office. It should be noted that these laws also applied to other groups such as the Romani and black people. These horrific conditions were worsened in 1938, when German Jews had their passports invalidated and were issued with replacements that had been stamped with the letter 'J'. This became a key mechanism of identification once the Nazis began the systematic eradication of Jewish people through extermination camps.

A key turning point in the path towards the Holocaust was Kristallnacht (often referred to as the 'Night of Broken Glass'), a symbolic escalation of physical violence towards Jews in Germany that occurred on 9 and 10 November 1938. This was a pogrom (a riot directed towards a particular ethnic or religious group) that saw violent attacks on the property of German Jews. Following Kristallnacht, the German government made laws that further deprived Jewish people of property and their means of livelihood and expelled Jewish children from German schools.

While they were consolidating and legalising the systematic persecution of Jewish people, the Nazis sought to 'educate' the people of Germany through propaganda, a task that Joseph Goebbels was appointed to coordinate. Goebbels portrayed Hitler as a saviour of Germany, building a cult of personality around the Führer through media such as newspapers, film and radio. Germans were expected to share the greeting 'Heil Hitler' as an expression of German loyalty. Meanwhile, the school curriculum was adapted not only to praise the leadership of Hitler, but also to perpetuate anti-Semitic attitudes.

World War II begins

As shocking as the events of the 1930s under Nazi rule were, the international community failed to speak out in support of German Jews. Furthermore, as key European powers, especially France and Britain, maintained a policy of appeasement, they failed to take any action as Nazi Germany revoked the limitations on its military that had been imposed by the Treaty of Versailles, and annexed (appropriated the territory of) Austria in March 1938. However, two days after Hitler's army invaded Poland from the west on 1 September 1939, France and Britain declared war on Germany. The invasion of Poland demonstrated the overwhelming military power that Germany had amassed.

The Holocaust

The term Holocaust is used to describe the Nazi regime's systematic persecution and murder of six million Jewish people during World War II. This act of genocide did not begin with a specific plan to gas Jews and others in concentration camps. Rather, it was a staged process that evolved over time, from identification and confinement in ghettos to mass shootings of Jewish communities, before reaching its culmination in the horrific apparatus for the systematic murder of people on an industrial scale (what was referred to as 'the Final Solution').

Identification and ghettos

The origins of the Holocaust can be traced to the Nazi policy forcing Jews to wear a badge or armband bearing the Star of David, used both to humiliate Jewish people and segregate them from the rest of the population. The Nazis used the war as a justification for further measures against Jews, particularly in Poland. The Jewish people were confined to ghettos, parts of the city where minority groups were forced to live and subjected to involuntary labour. Many died from disease or starvation due to the horrific conditions; it is estimated that approximately 800 000 Jews died in the ghettos.

Mass shootings

As the army of Nazi Germany marched through Eastern Europe, paramilitary death squads known as *Einsatzgruppen* were charged with neutralising political enemies. These squads killed any civilians that were perceived as enemies, shooting thousands of Jews. The frequency of these actions increased dramatically after Hitler ordered an advance against the Soviet Union in June 1941. It is important to note that many of these killings were not just done by the *Einsatzgruppen*. There were often local collaborators who helped to identify and kill victims, who were typically rounded up, marched or transported to a killing site, and forced to dig a mass grave. They would then be stripped of clothing and valuables, forced into the grave, then shot. It is estimated that at least 1.5 million Jews were murdered during this very public phase of the Holocaust.

The Final Solution

Mass shootings were resource intensive. The decision was therefore made to adopt the Euthanasia Program that had been used to kill severely handicapped or mentally ill people before the war as part of the quest to create a 'pure' Aryan race (which, in Nazi eyes, was non-Jewish Caucasian of Nordic appearance). Between 1941 and 1944, the Germans and their allies deported Jews from across Europe to extermination camps located in German-occupied Poland. In these centres, poison gas was the primary means utilised to murder groups of people en masse. It is estimated that nearly 2.7 million Jews were murdered at the five killing centres: Belzec, Chelmno, Sobibor, Treblinka and Auschwitz-Birkenau. Auschwitz-Birkenau, often referred to simply as Auschwitz, was the largest killing centre, with four gas chambers in operation.

Upon arrival at the killing centres, people were subjected to a selection process. Families were separated, with men and older boys in one column, and women and children of both sexes in the other. They were then judged by camp doctors and other officials who determined on sight whether those people would live or die. It is important to recognise that age was a key selection criteria. Children below sixteen years of age and the elderly were sent to die immediately. It should be noted that the survival of Shmuel in *The Boy in the Striped Pyjamas* was therefore highly improbable.

Prisoner uniforms

The standard issue uniforms used by the Nazi regime for prisoners in concentration camps were made of coarse grey-blue striped material. These uniforms were marked with badges indicating a prisoner's category and an identification number that replaced their name. It is this uniform that Bruno refers to as 'striped pyjamas' in the novel.

The end of World War II

As the Allied forces moved across Europe in a series of offensives against Germany in the final months of the war in Europe, the Germans forced many inmates of the camps onto trains or to undertake forced marches (also known as death marches), to prevent them being liberated by the Allies. These marches continued until 7 May 1945 when German forces surrendered unconditionally to the Allies, with World War II in Europe officially ending on 8 May 1945 on what is referred to as VE (Victory in Europe) Day.

GENRE, STRUCTURE & LANGUAGE

Genre

Historical fiction

The Boy in the Striped Pyjamas is classified as historical fiction. This is a literary genre in which the reader is transported to another time and place (either real or imagined) that draws upon real people and events. Boyne uses the setting of Auschwitz to locate the narrative both chronologically and geographically, and also incorporates characters who are actual historical figures such as 'the Fury' (Adolf Hitler) and Eva Braun.

Fable

Boyne describes *The Boy in the Striped Pyjamas* as a fable. Fables are stories that teach moral lessons, so in labelling his novel thus, Boyne makes it clear that he is taking a position on issues addressed within the story. In an interview in 2006 for the website bookreporter, Boyne explained:

> Considering the serious subject matter of this novel and the fact that I would be taking certain aspects of concentration camp history and changing them slightly in order to serve the story, I felt it was important not to pretend that a story like this was fully based in reality (which was also the reason why I chose never to use the word 'Auschwitz' in the novel). My understanding of the term 'fable' is a piece of fiction that contains a moral. (Bookreporter.com 2006)

Boyne uses the fable form to give voice to the nature of the atrocities of the Holocaust. He does so in the hope that his story may contribute to honouring the memory of those who lost their lives, as well as to prevent a repetition of such horrors, even though, as Boyne himself suggests in an interview that appears after the end of the novel, 'the fences that divide the adults in the novel ... continue to exist around the world today' (pp.236–7).

Structure

The novel is structured into twenty chapters that are primarily chronological in order. There are some flashbacks as Bruno recalls key moments from when he and his family lived in Berlin (such as in Chapter 8, p.89). Boyne utilises the title of each chapter to provide an indication of its focus. For example, Chapter 4, 'What They Saw Through the Window', explores Bruno and Gretel's first impression of the camp that they see through Bruno's bedroom window, while Chapter 13, 'The Bottle of Wine', foreshadows the shocking beating of Pavel by Lieutenant Kotler for spilling wine while serving the family.

Narrative voice

The novel is written in the third person, primarily from the limited perspective of nine-year-old Bruno. The narrative voice of Bruno conveys a complete absence of comprehension of the world in which he lives. Bruno's naivety is essential for the denouement of the novel to have its impact and also allows for Boyne to warn his readers of the dangers of ignorance and metaphorical blindness.

Foreshadowing

Boyne relies upon the reader having some awareness of the events of the Holocaust so that they can see the inherent danger of Bruno's decision to crawl under the fence 'to see what was really on the other side' (p.205). It is the reader's understanding of the Holocaust that indicates to them that, with this fateful decision, death is now likely.

Language

Dramatic irony

Much of the irony in Boyne's novel is dependent upon the reader's understanding of the history of the events of the Holocaust. Advance knowledge of specific elements of the Holocaust is needed to understand the irony of Bruno's observations. Thus, when Bruno tells Shmuel that his train to Out-With was only unpleasant because 'you all crowded onto one train' (p.133), the reader is painfully aware that Shmuel had no choice, and that he was transported in intolerable conditions.

Malapropisms

Malapropism is the mistaken use of a word in place of a similar sounding one. Bruno employs a number of malapropisms that represent the fog of naivety that dominates his existence. The mispronunciation of Auschwitz as 'Out-With' and the Führer as 'the Fury' suggests that these are words that he has overheard, but perhaps has never been explicitly told the meaning and significance of. It should be noted that these malapropisms are illogical and implausible – Bruno's native language is German and he would have been explicitly educated about the Führer in school. While these malapropisms are illogical, they are an essential tool used by Boyne to accentuate Bruno's innocence and ignorance.

Metonyms and symbols

A metonym is a figure of speech in which one object or idea takes the place of another that has a close association. When writing about the Holocaust, symbols such as trains and fences become signifiers of something bigger and truly horrific. For example, the fence that marks the divide between Out-With and Bruno's home signifies the division between the Germans and the Jews – on one side of the fence is starvation and suffering, on the other, prosperity and privilege.

Window frames limit the view of the camp from the house, symbolising the children's limited understanding of Out-With. This is most evident when they peer through the window of Bruno's bedroom and see an image that confuses them:

> Everywhere they looked they could see people ... Some were formed into a sort of chain gang and pushing wheelbarrows from one side of the camp to the other, appearing from a place out of sight and taking their wheelbarrows further along behind a hut, where they disappeared again. (p.37)

Note how, in this excerpt, the people move in and out of the frame. This implies that the children have a limited view of the world around them, thereby highlighting the dangers of ignorance.

Motifs

A motif is a symbolic image or idea that appears frequently in a story. They can be actions, sounds, words, symbols or ideas, and they contribute to the reader's understanding of the themes presented in the narrative. There are many motifs in *The Boy in the Striped Pyjamas*, some of which are described below.

Boundaries, both literal and metaphorical, surround Bruno. The fence that separates him from the camp is the most obvious one. Another example is Father's office, repeatedly referred to by Bruno as 'Out Of Bounds At All Times And No Exceptions'. The capitalisation here suggests that this had been said to Bruno repeatedly, creating a physical and emotional barrier in the relationship with his father.

Bruno's love of **adventure** is clearly established from the beginning of the narrative. He has an active imagination and loves to explore. He also loves *Treasure Island*, Robert Louis Stevenson's famous adventure novel, which feeds his interest in exploration. This passion for adventure sees Bruno follow the fence line where he finds Shmuel, and ultimately go under it and towards his death.

Clothing is significant. To understand the importance of the striped pyjamas worn by the prisoners, one should trace the way they are encountered by Bruno throughout the novel. Initially, they are something seen only from a distance, a piece of clothing signifying the idea of Jewish otherness that Nazi propaganda sought to generate. The pyjamas are an emblem of the destruction of the identity of Jewish people in the camps. However, as the novel progresses, Bruno's friendship with Shmuel allows him to see beyond the clothing and to get to know the person, while his final donning of the clothes himself becomes a symbol of his bond of friendship with Shmuel. His demise also reminds the reader of what the striped pyjamas ultimately meant: death for anyone who was caught up in the cruel Nazi program of eradication.

Boyne builds upon this idea of the importance of clothing through Bruno's observations of the uniforms worn by the Nazi soldiers, and Father in particular. While Father and most of the family are proud of this uniform, Grandmother observes that he is 'dressing up like a puppet on a string' (p.94). This quote suggests that the uniforms are simply a tool utilised by the Nazis to control the servants of the regime.

Doubling/Mirroring

Doubling is a feature that allows two things to be compared or contrasted. Literary doubling is used with the characters of Bruno and Shmuel, made explicit within the narrative as the boys discover they were 'born on the same day' and are therefore 'like twins' (p.113). This invites the reader to draw a comparison between the two boys and reflect on the cruelty that sees two children, alike in so many ways, separated and treated so differently due to the prejudice of adults.

CHAPTER-BY-CHAPTER ANALYSIS

Chapter 1: Bruno Makes a Discovery (pp.1–11)

Summary: *Berlin, Germany, circa 1942. Bruno arrives home to find his belongings being packed by the maid, Maria. Mother tells him they are moving, which makes him unhappy.*

The narrative voice of nine-year-old Bruno is immediately youthful and naive. Upon hearing that he and his family are to move, his childish self-interest dominates his thoughts – he hopes that his sister will not join them because she is a 'Hopeless Case' (p.3), yet he is upset that he will leave behind Karl, Daniel and Martin, his 'three best friends for life' (p.8). Bruno only knows Father's job is 'very important' (p.5) because Mother tells him so; he confesses to the reader that 'if he was honest with himself – which he always tried to be – he wasn't entirely sure what job Father did' (p.4). This ignorance is a barrier to Bruno understanding the cruel nature of Father's work.

Bruno's naivety is in part due to the way he is parented. Mother silences him, declaring 'that's enough questions for now' (p.6) and simply repeats that Father has 'a very special job' (p.4), assuming her son has a level of knowledge that does not exist. Father is conspicuously absent in his son's life, spending most of his time in his office, which is 'Out Of Bounds At All Times And No Exceptions' (p.10). The capitalisation suggests this is a pronouncement delivered by Bruno's authoritarian father, indicating a substantial barrier to communication between father and son.

Father occupies a high-ranking position in the Nazi Party. The family have hosted 'the Fury' (p.3), understood to represent Adolf Hitler, while 'men in fantastic uniforms' and 'women with typewriters' come to their home and are 'very polite to Father' (p.4), suggesting that Father is a man to be feared.

Indirect characterisation conveys Mother's stress and agitation at the move and provides one of the first hints of her later unease when they reside in Out-With: Bruno observes that she is 'twisting her hands together nervously as if there was something she didn't want to have to say' (p.2) and that 'the rims of her eyes were more red than usual' (p.3). While Bruno does not understand the cause of his mother's unease, the fact that it is because 'we don't have a choice in this' (p.8) is clearly a core problem.

Key point

Bruno refers to 'the Fury' and 'the beautiful blonde woman who had come to dinner with the Fury' (p.3). These people are assumed by the informed reader to be Hitler, who used the title of Führer, and his girlfriend Eva Braun.

Q How does John Boyne successfully create Bruno's youthful voice? What features of his syntax can you observe?

Chapter 2: The New House (pp.12–21)

Summary: *Bruno dislikes his new home but is dismissed by his mother when he complains to her.*

Bruno's immediate response to his new home, in which his 'eyes opened wide, his mouth made the shape of an O and his arms stretched out at his sides' (p.12), indicates that something about the sight shocks him. Whereas Bruno lived a privileged life in Berlin, in 'a very beautiful house' that 'had five floors in total' (p.6), the new home is bleak. Boyne's diction conveys this: it is 'empty' and 'desolate' with 'no other boys to play with' (pp.12–13). It is described by Bruno as 'the loneliest place in the world' (p.14); the juxtaposition of this with images of abundance in Berlin where 'there were always people strolling along and stopping to chat' (p.13) positions the reader to concur with Bruno that his new home is no place for a child.

A sense of danger is generated by the activity in the household. Bruno notes that there are additional servants 'who were quite skinny and … spoke … in whispering voices' (p.14), while Maria also seems fearful, especially in the presence of Lieutenant Kotler, in front of whom she 'stared down at the ground … as if she was afraid she might be turned to stone if she looked directly at him' (p.20). Mother exudes a sense of disquiet, silencing her son's complaints by telling him, 'We don't have the luxury of thinking' because of 'some people' (p.15), and that they must simply tolerate their new home 'for the foreseeable future' (p.16). Bruno also senses danger and is distressed: he experiences 'a pain in his stomach' and feels he might 'shout and scream' or 'burst into tears' (p.16). This is not helped by the presence of Lieutenant Kotler, who 'looked the boy up and down as if he had never seen a child before and wasn't quite sure [whether to] eat it, ignore it or kick it down the stairs' (p.19). All of these elements imply that there is an ever-present threat of violence.

Q Explain the implication of Mother's statement, 'We don't have the luxury of thinking.'

Chapter 3: The Hopeless Case (pp.22–30)

Summary: *Bruno and Gretel discuss their new home. They look out of Bruno's window and are shocked by what they see.*

Although Bruno considers his sister to be a 'Hopeless Case' and is 'a little scared of her' (p.22), he goes into her room to speak with her. The children's conversation reveals that Mother and Father have failed to clearly speak to their children about their new life: the children misinterpret the statement that they 'would be here for the foreseeable future' (p.25) to mean only weeks. Their ignorance bodes dangerously for the future, especially when it emerges that they have no comprehension of what occurs on the other side of the fence. Gretel assumes a sense of superiority over her brother as she informs him that 'Out-With' is 'the name of the house' (p.26), utilising the same malapropism as her brother. Yet when he asks Gretel what the name means, her response that it means 'out with the people who lived here before us, I expect' (p.26) reveals her ignorance.

The children's conversation turns to their friends in Berlin, whom they both miss, until Bruno shocks Gretel when he says, 'I don't think the other children look at all friendly' (p.27), referring to the children he can see through his window. While Gretel has a view of the driveway and a forest, Bruno's view is of something else. Boyne generates a sense of foreboding as Gretel swallows 'nervously' as she looks out Bruno's window and says 'a silent prayer that they would indeed be returning to Berlin in the foreseeable future' (p.30).

Q What do you think is the purpose of the mispronunciation of 'Out-With' throughout the story?

Key vocabulary

Complicit: involved with others in an activity that is unlawful or morally wrong.

Foreseeable future: at a time that is not long from now.

Chapter 4: What They Saw Through the Window (pp.31–40)

Summary: *Bruno and Gretel try to comprehend what they see outside the window.*

Before allowing the reader to share the full view that the children have out of the window, Boyne generates curiosity through descriptions of the more immediate setting. Gretel observes flowers in the front garden and finds it odd that the bench in the garden is 'turned to face the house – which, usually, would be a strange thing to do but on this occasion she could understand why' (p.32).

The vision the children are confronted with evokes a prison. There is 'a huge wire fence' with 'enormous bales of barbed wire' at the top, and 'no greenery anywhere' (p.33). Furthermore, there are people 'formed into a sort of chain gang' (p.37) and 'children huddled together and being shouted at by a group of soldiers' (p.38). Gretel seeks to create meaning by explaining it as 'the countryside' where people 'live and work and send all the food to feed us' (p.35), even though she acknowledges it is a 'nasty-looking place' (p.34). Bruno is able to convince his sister that this is incorrect, but that simply leaves the children struggling to understand what it is they are looking at.

Interestingly, there is a divergence in the children's attitudes. Gretel turns her gaze away from the camp, choosing to direct her focus on the 'decidedly nicer' view from her own window, and 'closing the door behind her' (p.39) to completely block the unwelcome sight. In other words, Gretel literally turns her back on the obvious evidence of the persecution of a group of people. In contrast, Bruno spends longer contemplating the sight outside his window. However, he too ultimately opts for 'turning away' (p.40) from the unwelcome sight. It could be argued that the children's actions are part of a trauma response, or they could be accused of willingly embracing ignorance.

Q Authors often withhold information from their readers. At the end of this chapter, what has the author left unresolved? Consider why Boyne has chosen to do this.

Key vocabulary

Chain gang: a group of prisoners chained together.

Chapter 5: Out Of Bounds At All Times And No Exceptions (pp.41–56)

Summary: *Bruno seeks answers about the people in the striped pyjamas from his father.*

This chapter provides significant insight into the historical and political context in which the novel is set. Firstly, in a flashback scene, Mother stands in the family home in Berlin for a final time before they leave for Out-With and says to herself, 'We should never have let the Fury come to dinner' (p.42). However, when Mother realises that Maria is standing behind her, she becomes panicked and defensive as she blurts, 'I didn't mean …' and 'I wasn't trying to suggest …' (p.42). This fear is because of the inherent danger in being critical of the Führer or the Nazi Party, and Mother realises that Maria could get her into a great deal of trouble.

The next insights come when the narrative returns to the present and Bruno goes to Father's office to seek answers. In spite of the obvious intimidation he feels, Bruno dares to express his dislike of their new home. Father's responses speak to the political functioning of the Nazi Party, which did not tolerate challenges to authority. He instructs his son that 'sometimes there are things we need to do in life that we don't have a choice in' (p.50) and that Bruno needs to learn, as he did, 'when to keep [his] mouth shut and follow orders' (p.52). Rather than answer his son's intelligent and pertinent questions, Father instead denies him knowledge, continuing to speak in vague terms and ultimately silencing Bruno with the imperative, 'you will be quiet now' (p.53). When Bruno asks who the people on the other side of the fence are, Father simply responds with: 'they're not people at all' and 'you have nothing whatsoever in common with them' (p.55). The chapter concludes with Bruno returning the Nazi salute his father gives him and repeating the words '*Heil Hitler*' (p.56), despite not understanding their true significance.

Key point

Bruno's experience on the train platform gives the reader a glimpse of the transportation of Jewish people from their homes to the various extermination camps scattered across Poland. Boyne uses juxtaposition to show the way Jews are treated: they are surrounded by soldiers and bunched into 'crowds' (p.43), while Bruno and his family are escorted to the station in an 'official car with red-and-black flags' (p.42) that marks them as high-ranking Nazis.

Q Bruno's train has 'very few people on it and plenty of empty seats' while another train that also 'pointed eastwards' (p.43) has crowds of people on it. Why is this significant?

Q Father tells Bruno that he is successful because he 'learned when to argue and when to keep [his] mouth shut and follow orders' (p.52). What does this suggest about Father's personality and ethics?

Chapter 6: The Overpaid Maid (pp.57–68)

Summary: *Bruno and Maria talk after she overhears Bruno expressing his frustration when he thinks he is alone. Gretel commands Maria to run a bath for her.*

Bruno's hatred of his new home is evident in his belief that 'nothing … not even the insects, would ever choose to stay at Out-With' and his repetitious use of the word 'hate' (pp.57–8) as he vocalises his feelings when he believes he is alone. When Maria enters the room, Bruno tries to get her to express a shared hatred of this place, but she maintains her silence. Boyne utilises Maria's response to show how fear can drive people to remain silent, even in the face of terrible atrocities. Maria seems to struggle to determine what to say and then is evasive, speaking of what she misses about Berlin rather than speaking ill of the new home. Maria recognises that speaking against the regime could have terrible consequences for her if word got back to the Commandant. In contrast to Bruno, who seeks answers and sees that something is not right,

Maria maintains wilful ignorance, turning a blind eye to what Father is overseeing and instead insisting to Bruno that his father is 'a very good man' (p.61) who has 'a lot of kindness in his soul' (p.64). She encourages Bruno to do the same and 'just keep quiet' and 'do whatever your father tells you ... until this is all over' (p.67).

Key point

Gretel's behaviour towards Maria, when she imperiously commands her to run a bath for her, mimics that of her Father in his interactions with those beneath him in rank. This small moment reveals how children can learn prejudice and hate from those around them, especially their parents. As she transitions to adulthood, Gretel demonstrates more of these malicious attributes.

Q What are the consequences of people maintaining their silence like Maria does?

Key vocabulary

Prejudice: a preconceived opinion that is not based on reason or experience.

Chapter 7: How Mother Took Credit for Something That She Hadn't Done (pp.69–88)

Summary: *Bruno decides to build a tyre swing. Lieutenant Kotler orders Pavel to get a tyre for Bruno. Bruno falls from the swing and injures himself and Pavel cares for him. Mother takes credit for cleaning Bruno's wounds.*

Although he does so 'without much enthusiasm' (p.73) because of his dislike of Lieutenant Kotler, Bruno asks for his help in locating a tyre to make a swing. Kotler directs Pavel to help Bruno. Bruno is shocked by the cruel manner in which Kotler speaks to Pavel, repeatedly calling him by a name 'that Bruno did not understand' but 'made Bruno look away and feel ashamed to be part of this at all' (p.78). His instinctive repudiation of Kotler's anti-Semitic persecution of Pavel reveals that Bruno has an innate sense of right and wrong that has not yet been tainted by the toxic ideology of the Nazis.

Bruno falls off his swing and suffers a blow to the head and a wide gash on his knee. Both Mother and Father are absent, so Pavel comes to his aid. Pavel is characterised as a gentle and caring man, scooping Bruno up and speaking 'in a quiet voice that immediately made Bruno feel safe' (p.81). Despite the danger such a revelation poses, Pavel tells Bruno he was a doctor before being transported to Out-With, and tends to Bruno's injuries. Pavel's gentle insistence on his identity prompts Bruno to 'look at him closely for the first time' (p.85) and consider that there is more to this man than peeling potatoes. This brief encounter reveals that Bruno is open to communicating with others, in a clear foreshadowing of his future friendship with Shmuel.

To Bruno's disgust, when Mother arrives home she tells Pavel: 'If the Commandant asks, we'll say that I cleaned Bruno up' (p.88). While Bruno thinks that this is Mother being 'terribly selfish' (p.88), it suggests she has some sense of compassion and kindness, for she is protecting Pavel from the harsh retribution that he would no doubt receive if it was made known that he had laid hands on Bruno.

Q Contrast the characterisation of Pavel with that of Lieutenant Kotler, and explain how this helps to develop Boyne's themes.

Key vocabulary

Anti-Semitism: prejudice against or hatred of Jews.

Ideology: a system of ideas and ideals, especially one that forms the basis of economic or political theory and policy.

Chapter 8: Why Grandmother Stormed Out (pp.89–97)

Summary: *Bruno recalls the family Christmas the year before. Back in the present, he writes a letter to Grandmother.*

The chapter begins with Bruno thinking about his grandparents, who have remained in Berlin. Bruno recalls with fondness the plays Grandmother would write to perform with him and Gretel at Christmas. These memories prompt Bruno to recall 'the last play they had performed', which 'ended in disaster' (p.92). The news that Father has been promoted to the role of Commandant following a visit to the house by 'the Fury and the beautiful blonde woman' (p.92) is shared, and all are encouraged to congratulate Father. Notably, Bruno 'wasn't entirely sure what he was congratulating him for' (p.93): this reinforces the extent of Bruno's ignorance. The diverging responses of Grandmother and Grandfather to Father's promotion are important. Whereas Grandfather is 'very proud' (p.93) of his son because he is 'helping [Germany] reclaim her pride after all the great wrongs that were done to her' (p.95), Grandmother is 'unimpressed' (p.93) and 'ashamed' (p.96). She challenges Father's insistence that he is 'a patriot' (p.96) and expresses disgust at what the uniform 'stands for' (p.94) and the 'terrible, terrible things' he does (p.96). Importantly, her simile when she says Father is 'dressing up like a puppet on a string' (p.94) implies that Father does not actually have any control, and is simply acting in accordance with the demands of his master, the Führer.

The chapter concludes with a return to the present as Bruno writes a letter to his Grandmother telling her 'about the people living there and their striped pyjamas and cloth caps, and … how much he missed her' (p.97), suggesting that Bruno is struggling to cope with the traumatic sights that he bears witness to through his window, as well as the loneliness of his new home.

Q Discuss why regimes such as that of Nazi Germany emphasise the importance of uniforms.

Chapter 9: Bruno Remembers That He Used to Enjoy Exploration (pp.98–106)

Summary: *Many months pass. Father decides that Bruno and Gretel should have a tutor. Bruno goes exploring even though it is forbidden.*

Bruno continues to feel lonely and bored. Gretel is 'less than friendly' (p.98), while Mother seems to spend a lot of time with Lieutenant Kotler 'whispering alone in rooms' (p.99), implying there may be an inappropriate relationship forming.

The children begin lessons with a tutor, Herr Liszt, who is 'particularly fond of history and geography' (p.100). Herr Liszt's lessons emphasise the 'great wrongs' committed against 'the Fatherland' (p.101) – a reference to the Treaty of Versailles. Such lessons are crucial for indoctrinating the children.

Bruno's boredom leads him to recollect that he 'used to enjoy exploring' (p.102), and he reflects on all that he has witnessed at Out-With and 'wonder[s] what it was all about' (p.103). In spite of the repeated instructions from both Mother and Father that Bruno 'was not allowed to walk in this direction, that he was not allowed anywhere near the fence or the camp', and that 'exploration was banned at Out-With' (p.106), Bruno makes the fateful decision to go exploring. This decision is a consequence of his ignorance – his parents have sought to shelter him from the unpleasant realities of what is going on and so he is unaware of the full extent of the danger posed within the camp.

Key point

There is an illogical disconnect in this point of the narrative: Bruno wonders if the people on the other side of the fence were 'really so different' (p.103), yet Herr Liszt's lessons would have utilised the educational propaganda designed to indoctrinate German children and poison their minds against Jewish people. Bruno's continued ignorance could be a symptom of him trying to process the trauma of what he has witnessed. Alternatively, he is simply more like his grandmother, who is unwilling to buy into the pseudoscientific arguments of racial superiority used by the Nazis.

Q What evidence is there that Herr Liszt resents the penalties Germany incurred after World War I?

Key vocabulary

Boneshaker: a dilapidated, uncomfortable or outdated vehicle.

Chapter 10: The Dot That Became a Speck That Became a Blob That Became a Figure That Became a Boy (pp.107–18)

Summary: *Bruno goes exploring and discovers Shmuel sitting on the other side of the fence. The boys strike up a friendship.*

The title of this chapter bears significance as it implies that Bruno's vision is being brought into focus: Shmuel goes from being a 'dot' to a 'speck' to a 'blob' to a 'figure' and finally, and significantly, to a 'person' (p.108). This key turning point in the narrative drives the action of the remainder of the novel. Boyne's description of Shmuel brings to attention the living conditions at Out-With; his skin, 'almost the colour of grey', and his 'enormous pair of sad eyes' (p.110) indicate that he is malnourished and that he has witnessed unimaginable atrocities. Furthermore, the Jewish star on his armband signifies the identification process that was used to isolate and persecute Jewish people.

Boyne uses mirroring in this chapter to emphasise the boys' common humanity. They discover that they share the same birthday, and Bruno sits 'down on the ground on his side of the fence … like the little boy' (p.111). Bruno's claim that the two boys are 'like twins' (p.113) is sweet yet inaccurate; while the boys share many similarities, their separation by the fence marks a clear difference between them: Bruno experiences freedom, while Shmuel suffers confinement. Bruno's ignorance and his indoctrination from his lessons with Herr Liszt become obvious. He has no idea where Poland is yet claims 'that's not as good as Germany' and declares that 'Germany is the greatest of all countries' (p.115). Yet it also seems that Bruno is not quite convinced by his lessons, for 'even as he had said the words, they didn't sound quite right to him' (p.115). The chapter concludes with Bruno asking Shmuel the question that has been occupying his mind for some time: 'Why are there so many people on that side of the fence ... And what are you all doing there?' (p.118). Bruno has not been satisfied by his father's previous dismissive claim that 'they're not people at all' (p.55).

Key point

Shmuel's claim that 'there are a lot of us – boys our age, I mean – on this side of the fence' (p.114) is a point for which Boyne is often criticised, as young boys would typically be sent directly to the gas chambers during the selection process upon arrival. Boyne is clear that there are some historical inaccuracies like this in his narrative, as they help in achieving his authorial purpose.

Q How does Boyne encourage the reader to feel concern for Shmuel's wellbeing?

Chapter 11: The Fury (pp.119–28)

Summary: *A flashback to months before the family moved from Berlin, when the Fury and his girlfriend came to dinner, is described.*

Father's announcement that the Fury has 'invited himself to dinner' (p.120) sends the house into a flurry of preparation. The children are dressed up in new clothes to impress the guests, and Father sets strict rules for the children to ensure they 'show [Hitler] the respect and courtesy that such a great leader deserves' (p.123). Interestingly, when Bruno asks, 'Who's the Fury?', Father refuses to believe his son is that ignorant, declaring 'You know perfectly well who the Fury is' (p.120).

Boyne characterises Bruno as having good instincts and a natural goodness about him through Bruno's immediate dislike of the Fury, who is 'the rudest guest [he] had ever witnessed' (p.125).

Following the departure of the guests, Bruno overhears Mother and Father fighting about his new post as Commandant at Out-With. The exchange hints that Mother does not agree with the actions of the

Nazis, and is horrified that they are being sent to 'such a place' (p.127). However, in a clear indication of the power Father has, both because he is the family patriarch and because of his professional rank, he silences Mother and declares 'an end to the matter' (p.128), thereby demanding her blind obedience.

Chapter 12: Shmuel Thinks of an Answer to Bruno's Question (pp.129–37)

Summary: *Bruno and Shmuel talk at the fence. Shmuel explains his life before he came to Out-With, which Bruno struggles to understand.*

Shmuel's recollection of his experiences draws a distressing (though sanitised) picture of what happened to so many Jewish victims of the Holocaust. Moved from their home to a ghetto in Cracow (also spelled Kraków), the family were forced to wear armbands that bore the Jewish star 'every time [they] left the house' (p.130) and then were transported to Out-With on trains, where the men and women were separated and their possessions taken from them. Bruno seems convinced 'it didn't seem like such a terrible thing' as 'after all much the same thing had happened to him' (p.134) – this exposes his persistent ignorance. He notes that Father also wears an armband, although it bears a different symbol (the swastika), and even complains, 'No one's ever given me an armband' (p.130). Whereas Bruno naively sees the armbands as symbols of belonging, Shmuel associates them with imprisonment and cruelty because of his experiences in the camp. The conversation between the boys reinforces that they are narrative doubles, but also serves to highlight the vast differences in their experiences and to accentuate Bruno's ignorance of (or wilful blindness to) what is happening around him. The chapter also highlights the depth of the trauma experienced by Jewish people during the Holocaust and encourages the reader to feel sympathy for their plight.

Q At the end of the chapter, Bruno decides that it 'might not be a good idea' (p.136) to tell his family about his new friend. List the possible reasons why.

Chapter 13: The Bottle of Wine (pp.138–54)

Summary: *Bruno is settling into his life at Out-With, due in large part to his friendship with Shmuel. Maria and Bruno talk about Pavel. Information about Kotler's father is revealed. Pavel is beaten by Kotler.*

Each afternoon, Bruno sets out to meet Shmuel. Before departing to see Shmuel one day, Bruno asks Maria a question 'that had been bothering him for some time' (p.139): why Pavel said he was a doctor. Maria's explanation that Pavel was a doctor 'in another life' (p.141) encapsulates how Jewish people were stripped of their identities when processed in the concentration camps. In addition, Maria's insistence that he 'mustn't tell anyone' (p.141) what they know of Pavel's life evinces (shows clearly) the danger of challenging the Nazi program of dehumanisation and extermination of Jewish people.

When Bruno arrives to see Shmuel, he passes to his friend 'the bits that he hadn't already eaten on the way' (p.142). Although bringing the food is an act of friendship, the act of eating some of it reinforces Bruno's ignorance and selfishness. The boys' conversation turns to soldiers. While Bruno exhibits some understanding of the persecution of the Jewish prisoners when he says 'if Father had known that [Pavel] had cleaned my knee ... there would have been trouble' (p.143), he also still seeks to deny the truth of what his father is capable of, insisting that Father is 'one of the good soldiers' (p.144). This ironic claim is refuted by Shmuel who repeats, 'There aren't any good soldiers' (p.144), but Bruno ignores the obvious and mounting evidence of his Father's role. The conversation turns to Lieutenant Kotler, whom Shmuel confesses 'scares me' (p.145). When Shmuel starts 'to shiver slightly' (p.145), Boyne implies that Shmuel has witnessed Kotler's cruelty first-hand.

At dinner Bruno notices that Pavel, like Shmuel, 'seemed to grow smaller and smaller each week' (p.146) and that 'his hands were shaking slightly' (p.147). Both Pavel and Shmuel are presented to the readers as examples of the cruel starvation of the Jewish prisoners in the camps, and Boyne uses Bruno's concerned tone to garner the reader's compassion for the suffering experienced. As the dinner conversation turns to the children's studies, it emerges that Kotler's father was 'a professor of literature' and 'left Germany some years ago' in 1938 (p.149). The mood becomes dangerous; Kotler sits stiffly and avoids making eye contact, becoming nervous when Father asks probing questions. Father's comment, 'Strange that he chose not to stay in the Fatherland' (p.150), is ominous, and when he suggests that Kotler's father had 'disagreements' (p.151) and labels such people as 'disturbed', 'traitors' and 'cowards' he reveals the truth of how the Nazis maintained power – through bullying, intimidation and labelling anyone who disagreed with them as criminals.

The scene concludes with the implied brutal beating of Pavel by Kotler for spilling wine on him. Kotler's actions could in part be considered a performance for his Commandant to prove his loyalty to Nazi ideology, yet it seems such violence by the young soldier is common. Most telling is the silence of all at the table; nobody 'stepped in to stop him ... even though none of them could watch' (p.153). This moment is doubly significant. First, it is direct evidence that those who sit silently while atrocities are committed are complicit in the act. Secondly, it teaches Bruno that 'he would do well to keep his mouth shut' (p.153).

Chapter 14: Bruno Tells a Perfectly Reasonable Lie (pp.155–65)

Summary: *On a rainy afternoon, Bruno accidently speaks of Shmuel to Gretel. He covers it up by pretending Shmuel is an imaginary friend.*

While Bruno and Shmuel continue to share stories, each seems to avoid some topics. Shmuel does not go into detail about his experiences, such as why he has a black eye one day, because he wants to 'pretend it had never happened' (p.156). At the same time, Bruno still complains about his own life, and refuses to acknowledge how horrific conditions are on Shmuel's side of the fence; he even ironically complains that it isn't fair because 'Shmuel and his friends got to wear striped pyjamas all day long' (p.157). While the evasions and silences of both boys are clear signs of trauma, their strengthening bond is evident as Bruno feels 'an urge to help his friend' (p.155).

Days later, it is raining so Bruno cannot go out to meet Shmuel and he lets slip to Gretel that he 'should be with Shmuel by now' (p.159). The panic that Bruno immediately feels has two potential sources. The first could be his selfish desire to keep Shmuel to himself because he is '*his* friend and not hers and he didn't want to share him' (p.160). However, given the 'pain in his stomach' (p.159) that he feels in that moment, it is possible Bruno also realises that he is putting his friend in great danger (an assumption made all the more likely given what happened to Pavel). To cover up, Bruno sacrifices his dignity by pretending Shmuel is an imaginary friend. Yet talking to Gretel opens Bruno's eyes. As he recalls all the things that Shmuel has told him his voice goes quiet, for he finally sees how terribly sad his friend is, and therefore how much he needs the support of a friend.

Q How does Shmuel react when Bruno starts talking about Kotler? Note down words and phrases that convey the mood.

Chapter 15: Something He Shouldn't Have Done (pp.166–81)

Summary: *Several weeks pass. Bruno notices Shmuel is getting very thin. Bruno discovers Shmuel cleaning glasses in the kitchen. Bruno gives Shmuel food, but Kotler catches Shmuel.*

Like Pavel, Shmuel is becoming increasingly thin and Bruno notes that 'his face was growing more and more grey' (p.166). Boyne accentuates the extent to which the Jewish prisoners are being starved to death by contrasting Shmuel's hand with Bruno's: while Bruno's hands are pink and full, he notices that Shmuel's 'was like the hand of [a] pretend skeleton' (p.172). When Shmuel tells Bruno that his hand 'used to look more like yours' and that 'everyone on my side of the fence looks like this now' (p.173), the reader infers just how horrific the conditions on the other side of the fence are.

The boys' friendship undergoes its greatest challenge when Bruno finds Shmuel in his kitchen polishing glasses in preparation for Father's birthday. Boyne once again characterises Bruno as a well-meaning yet dreadfully naive boy: when Bruno offers Shmuel some chicken, he cannot comprehend Shmuel's reluctance to take the proffered food despite how starved he is. The mood generated with the entrance of Kotler into the kitchen ensures the reader understands Shmuel's fear, as Bruno feels 'the atmosphere grow heavy, sensing Shmuel's shoulders sinking down' (p.176). Yet when Kotler challenges Shmuel for having eaten and looks to Bruno for an explanation, Bruno fails his friend. Even though Shmuel is 'terrified' and Bruno 'wanted to say the right thing to make things better' (p.177), Bruno finds himself incapable of moving or speaking in his friend's defence. The reason – he is 'just as terrified himself' (p.177). This moment gives a clear indication that Bruno may be suffering from trauma because of the things he has witnessed, particularly at the hands of Kotler.

Key point

The guilt that Bruno feels after the incident with Kotler, and his concern for his friend, reinforce that Bruno is, at heart, a good person. After a week of not showing up at the fence, Shmuel finally returns, bearing bruises caused by Kotler. Bruno's heartfelt apology ensures that he and Shmuel are able to reconnect. Shmuel reaches his hand under the fence and 'the two boys shook hands and smiled at each other' (p.181), touching for the first time. This is a highly symbolic moment – Boyne is asserting that true friendship can overcome any barriers, whether it be literal fences such as the one that separates the boys, or the metaphorical fences that we construct in society, such as prejudice.

Q What evidence is there in this chapter that Mother and Lieutenant Kotler may be having an affair?

Chapter 16: The Haircut (pp.182–91)

Summary: *A year has passed. Grandmother dies, so the family return to Berlin for two days. Kotler is moved away from Out-With. Bruno asks Gretel why the fence is there. Bruno's head is shaved after head lice are discovered.*

After almost a year at Out-With, the family return to Berlin for the funeral of Grandmother. The funeral demonstrates that, even for his own mother, Father is unable to set aside his nationalistic fervour. Even though Grandmother was outspoken in her disapproval of Nazi ideology, Father wears 'his most impressive uniform' and is 'proud of the fact' (p.183) that a wreath has been sent by the Fury. Mother is clearly critical of her husband's willingness to put his Nazism before all else, lamenting that 'Grandmother would turn in her grave' (p.183) at the Nazi presence at her funeral.

Back at Out-With, Bruno feels more content. One reason is the removal of Kotler, whose 'departure had come about very suddenly' after 'a lot of shouting between Father and Mother' (p.184). It is unclear whether Kotler's sudden disappearance is because of the revelation of Kotler's father's background, which Father had ominously warned would be followed up, or because of the young soldier's interactions with Mother. Regardless, the reader understands that Kotler has been removed at the instigation of Father, once again implying that he has the capacity to be cruel and punitive.

Bruno wants to understand why Shmuel and all the other 'striped pyjama' people are on the other side of the fence, so he asks his sister 'why it's there' (p.187). Gretel's response suggests that, in contrast to Bruno, Herr Liszt's lessons have been successful in indoctrinating her with the Nazi's nationalistic and anti-Semitic ideology. Gretel tells Bruno it is to keep Jewish people 'together … with their own kind' because 'they can't mix with us' (p.188). However, Gretel's inability to specify how the Jews differ from Germans highlights the absence of logic in the anti-Semitic rhetoric that sought to dehumanise Jewish people.

The chapter ominously concludes with Bruno's head being shaved because of the discovery of head lice. This fateful decision seals Bruno's subsequent fate. It is evident that Bruno associates the shaved head with fear and danger as he is 'almost scared of his own reflection' (p.191).

Key point

Bruno's observation that he 'couldn't help but think how much like Shmuel he looked now' (p.191) is a deliberate tool used to make the point that there is no difference between a Jewish child and a Nazi child, other than the arbitrary and illogical differences imposed by society.

Q How has Gretel changed? Who or what has influenced her?

Chapter 17: Mother Gets Her Own Way (pp.192–8)

Summary: *After much arguing, Father agrees that Mother and the children can return to Berlin.*

While Bruno has settled into life at Out-With, in large part because his afternoon visits with Shmuel 'filled him with happiness' (p.194), Mother is experiencing obvious signs of depression because of her loneliness and isolation. She is 'having an awful lot more of her afternoon naps' and a lot of 'medicinal sherries' (p.194) to try to cope, and Bruno overhears his parents fighting behind closed doors. Mother's dislike for what her husband is overseeing is evident in her rhetorical question 'You call this work?' (p.193), implying that it is something else (that is, systematic murder). Father finally consents to Mother and the children returning to Berlin 'within the week' (p.198). This distresses Bruno as he is upset to be losing his best friend and 'dreaded having to tell Shmuel the news' (p.198).

Chapter 18: Thinking Up the Final Adventure (pp.199–206)

Summary: *Bruno tells Shmuel he is returning to Berlin. Shmuel's father has disappeared. The boys plan a 'final adventure'.*

When Bruno tells Shmuel that he is leaving, Shmuel is 'more unhappy than usual' (p.200) because he can't find his father who 'went on work duty with some other men and none of them have come back' (p.200). The reader can infer that he has been killed. Shmuel's unrealistic hope that he might be able to find his father heightens the pathos (emotional resonance) of this moment. Unbelievably, Bruno still remains ignorant of the 'work' that goes on in the camp, as evidenced by his suggestion that Father could help find Shmuel's father, when it is under Father's orders as Commandant that he would have died. It is clear that Shmuel is not as ignorant as Bruno, given his response, 'I don't think that would be a good idea' (p.201). Furthermore, for the first time the narrative links Father directly to the horrors in the camp through Shmuel's viewpoint: 'He had seen Bruno's father on any number of occasions and couldn't understand how such a man could have a son who was so friendly and kind' (p.202). However, Shmuel is so desperate to preserve his friendship with Bruno that he does not say this out loud.

After the boys express a shared desire to have had the opportunity to 'play together' (p.203), they hatch a plan that fills the informed reader with dread. Capitalising on the doubling motif developed throughout the novel, the boys reason that if Bruno were to wear the pyjamas then no one would be able to tell the difference between them, and so Bruno can help Shmuel explore the camp and find his father. Coupled with the allusion to the Final Solution in the chapter title, and the narrative claim that 'it seemed like a very sensible plan and a good way to say goodbye' (p.206), the demise of the boys is foreshadowed, and the reader is left to watch powerlessly as the tragedy comes to its conclusion.

Chapter 19: What Happened the Next Day (pp.207–20)

Summary: *Bruno and Shmuel go on their planned adventure. As the boys explore the camp they get caught up in a forced march.*

Boyne uses the weather to symbolise the approaching doom facing the boys. The day starts rainy and the sky remains overcast, until 'it started to get darker' (p.216) and the rain pours and thunder booms cataclysmically just as the boys are sent into the gas chamber. However, the weather is not enough to stop Bruno, who sees going under the fence as a great adventure and is excited by 'the prospect of exploring the world on the other side of the fence' (p.210). Bruno's ignorance and innocence has led him into great danger. This danger worsens when he puts on the 'disguise' (p.209) of the striped pyjamas and cap, which makes it 'difficult to tell [the boys] apart' (p.211).

The sights Bruno witnesses on the other side of the fence shock him – he had imagined 'huts ... full of happy families' (p.214) but instead all he sees is people who are 'terribly skinny' with 'sunken' eyes (p.215). Even confronted by these horrors, Bruno seems incapable of truly seeing the reality of what has been going on; when the boys are rounded up with Jewish prisoners to march into a gas chamber, Bruno 'wanted to whisper to them that everything was all right, that Father was the Commandant, and if this was the kind of thing that he wanted the people to do then it must be all right' (p.217). Bruno's wilful blindness to the atrocities that his father has been overseeing indicates that sometimes we embrace ignorance as a defence mechanism to avoid unwelcome truths.

Bruno's conscious decision to stay by his friend's side even though he doesn't 'like it here' (p.215) is testament to the strength of the bond the boys have formed. Bruno made a promise, and he keeps it. When the boys die together, holding hands for comfort, Boyne simultaneously reinforces their shared humanity, punishes Bruno's father for his role, and encourages the reader to reject any regime that would condone a system that allows for the death of innocence and innocents.

Q Bruno remembers something his grandmother once said: *'You wear the right outfit and you feel like the person you're pretending to be'* (p.212). How is this true for Bruno? What about his father? Why is this statement so important to the overall story?

Chapter 20: The Last Chapter (pp.221–3)

Summary: *Bruno has disappeared. Mother and Gretel return to Berlin. Father remains at Out-With until 'other soldiers' take him away.*

While the characters in the novel remain unaware of Bruno's fate, the reader understands that he has died anonymously, like so many millions of victims of the Holocaust, inhumanely cast away. For some time, Father cannot understand what has happened to his son until one day he works out the truth and 'his legs seemed to stop working right' (p.223). It can be assumed that Father realises how his own actions brought about his son's demise, hence why he goes with the Allied soldiers 'without complaint ... because he didn't really mind what they did to him any more' (p.223).

Boyne concludes the story in a deadpan (impassive or expressionless) tone as he ironically writes, 'And that's the end of the story about Bruno and his family. Of course all this happened a long time ago and nothing like that could ever happen again. Not in this day and age' (p.223). Boyne wants his reader to recognise the important lessons of his fable: that nationalism, racism and ignorance are dangers that we must always be alert to in order to avoid history repeating itself.

CHARACTERS & RELATIONSHIPS

Bruno

Key quotes

'Bruno, if you have any sense at all, you will stay quiet and concentrate on your school work and do whatever your father tells you.' (Maria, p.67)

'I used to enjoy exploring … I've never really done any exploring here. Perhaps it's time to start.' (Bruno, p.102)

Nine-year-old German boy Bruno is the protagonist of the novel. Boyne uses a third-person limited perspective, primarily from Bruno's point of view, to convey Bruno's ignorance, curiosity and deep capacity for empathy.

Bruno is obviously sheltered and naive. He seems to have little understanding that Germany is in the throes of war, focusing more on the fact that he has a house with 'five floors in total' (p.6) than that it is constantly filled with 'men in fantastic uniforms' and 'women with typewriters' (p.4) who obviously work for Father. Bruno's naivety persists throughout the novel, largely because his parents do little to ensure he has an adequate understanding of the turbulent and dangerous world in which he lives. He initially asks a lot of questions about their move and their new home, but Mother simply declares, 'We don't have a choice in this' (p.8), while Father responds with empty Nazi rhetoric: 'Those people … well, they're not people at all, Bruno' (p.55). The efforts at indoctrination are marginally successful. Bruno clearly takes in Herr Liszt's lessons in which he seeks to teach Bruno 'about the great wrongs that have been done' to him (p.101), for he subsequently parrots nationalistic propaganda to Shmuel, declaring that 'Germany is the greatest of all countries' and that Germans are 'superior' (p.115).

Central to Bruno's problem when they move to Out-With is his loneliness. With no peers to play with, and his family unwilling to give him the attention he needs, he goes in search of entertainment. When he remembers that he 'used to enjoy exploring' (p.102), his adventures lead him to Shmuel. In his conversations with Shmuel, Bruno is initially revealed to be self-centred. He is more concerned with having a friend to alleviate his boredom, and absurdly declares, 'It's so unfair' because he believes that Shmuel has 'dozens of friends' and is 'probably playing for hours every day' (p.114). This blindness in the face of overwhelming evidence persists. Even when Shmuel goes into the horrible details of how he and his family were first forced into ghettos and then sent to Out-With, Bruno cannot understand why Shmuel looks sad, thinking 'it didn't seem like such a terrible thing to him, and after all much the same thing had happened to him' (p.134). However, Shmuel satisfies Bruno's deep desire for companionship, and so he persists in seeking out the company of the small boy.

Bruno's empathy ultimately overrides his self-interest. He doesn't embrace the Nazi rhetoric, as his interactions first with Pavel and then with Shmuel have shown him the humanity of the people in the 'striped pyjamas'. This is why he asks, 'What exactly was the difference?' and 'who decided which people wore the striped pyjamas and which people wore the uniforms?' (p.103). Unfortunately, Bruno's continued failure to understand the answer to the second question is ultimately what leads to his death. His decision to dress up, thinking it is just an exciting opportunity to explore, leads to him dying at his best friend's side.

Key point

It is widely agreed that Bruno's ignorance regarding what goes on in the camp, and his lack of understanding of Nazi ideology, is unrealistic. However, Boyne's emphasis of Bruno's childish incomprehension is an important narrative tool as it simultaneously provides a safe distance between the young reader and the atrocities committed, while also driving the plot forward. Furthermore, it allows Boyne to highlight the dangers of being metaphorically blind to what is happening around us.

Shmuel

Key quotes

'"We're like twins," said Bruno. "A little bit," agreed Shmuel."' (p.113)
'It was almost (Shmuel thought) as if they were all exactly the same really.' (p.211)

From the moment Bruno encounters Shmuel, the titular 'boy in the striped pyjamas', the reader is given a strong authorial push to feel compassion and concern for the boy. The imagery is powerful: he bears 'a forlorn expression' (p.109), has 'an enormous pair of sad eyes' and his skin is 'almost the colour of grey' (p.110), signifying the malnourishment he is suffering in the camp. He serves as a character foil for Bruno, made obvious by Boyne's narrative construct of the boys sharing a birthday and being 'like twins' (p.113), as Bruno claims. However, Shmuel's response, 'a little bit' (p.113), to Bruno's claim is a signpost for the reader to consider the differences between the boys' experiences.

It is primarily through Shmuel that Bruno (and the reader) is given some insight into the persecution experienced by Jewish people throughout the Holocaust. While Bruno, in his self-centred fog of naivety, fails to truly listen to his new friend and comprehend his stories, the reader cannot ignore what has happened to Shmuel. He recalls being forced from his home, where he lived with his 'mother and father and [his] brother Josef' (p.129), into a ghetto in Cracow, where his family and another shared a single room. He recounts being required to wear an armband bearing the Jewish star, as well as the 'day the soldiers all came with huge trucks' (p.132) to take them to trains where there were 'many ... in the carriages' and 'no air to breathe' (p.133).

Friendship with Bruno offers Shmuel some brief respite from the harsh realities of life at Out-With. Shmuel seems to tolerate Bruno's insensitive complaining, and even forgives Bruno after he fails to support Shmuel's defence to Lieutenant Kotler that Bruno is his friend and gave him the chicken to eat. Shmuel's faith in his friend in this moment reminds the reader that he, too, is a child, and that in their innocence children sometimes put their faith in the wrong people. The poignant moment in which Bruno and Shmuel die clinging to each other's hands so tightly that 'nothing in the world' (p.220) would have persuaded them to let go is powerful because, as readers, we have become so invested in the wellbeing of these two boys that we hope that, as in a fairytale, they will ultimately be saved. But as Boyne so clearly wants the reader to understand, the Holocaust was not a fairytale, and very few escaped the brutalities of the Nazis.

Key point

Other than Pavel, with whom the reader (and Bruno) only has brief encounters, Shmuel is the only Jewish prisoner of the camp who is shown up close. The remainder of the people in the 'striped pyjamas' remain at the margins – glanced at, avoided and ignored. This reinforces the idea that few were aware of the full extent of the Final Solution, which was designed by the Nazis to remain a secret.

Gretel

Key quotes

'I'm going back to my room to arrange my dolls ... The view is decidedly nicer from there.' (Gretel, p.39)

'One afternoon a month or so earlier ... Gretel had decided that she didn't like dolls any more ... In their place she had hung up maps of Europe that Father had given her ...' (p.186)

Gretel is Bruno's twelve-year-old sister. Bruno calls Gretel a 'Hopeless Case' and believes that she causes 'nothing but trouble for him' (p.3). Gretel considers herself to be a great deal more mature than her brother, but Boyne makes it clear that she is still a child through her love of playing with her dolls. Like Bruno, Gretel feels lonely at Out-With and misses her best friends in Berlin. For this reason, she develops a childish crush on Lieutenant Kotler, observed by Bruno through the physical cues of 'laughing loudly and twirling her hair around her fingers' (p.74).

Initially, Gretel appears to be as naive as her brother about the purpose of Out-With, suggesting that Mother and Father have actively shielded their children from the darker aspects of the Nazi regime's ideology. However, Bruno still looks to her as a source of information to comprehend what happens on the other side of the fence. When Gretel looks at the view from Bruno's window for the first time, she struggles to understand what she sees as it is outside her realm of experience. She acknowledges it is 'a nasty-looking place' (p.34) but seems determined to ignore the truth of what is going on over there, first suggesting it must be 'our holiday home' (p.35) before ultimately deciding to go back to her own room because 'the view is decidedly nicer from there' (p.39). This conscious act of turning a blind eye to the obvious atrocities going on in the camp run by her father contrasts with Bruno's innate curiosity and desire to ask questions.

Gretel's maturation is signified by her transferring her interest from her dolls to the geography and movement of the war. In contrast to her brother, Gretel absorbs Herr Liszt's lessons, which are specifically designed to indoctrinate the children. As a result, when Bruno seeks to understand more about the people on the other side of the fence, Gretel parrots Nazi ideology, simplistically declaring that they are kept on the other side of the fence because they're Jews and 'they can't mix with us' but should instead be 'with their own kind' (p.188). Gretel can therefore be considered a representative of the many millions of people during the war who accepted Nazi propaganda and ignored what were obviously immoral acts.

Father

Key quotes

'Do you think that I would have made such a success of my life if I hadn't learned when to argue and when to keep my mouth shut and follow orders? Well, Bruno? Do you?' (Father, p.52)

'We are correcting history here.' (Father, p.148)

Bruno's father, Ralf, is characterised as a strict man who is unavailable to his children both emotionally and physically (signified by his office being 'Out Of Bounds At All Times And No Exceptions', p.46). It is Father's promotion to the role of Commandant of Out-With that forces the family to move there, and while his presence looms large over the narrative, he features very rarely, indicating how remiss he is in concerning himself with the wellbeing of his wife and children. When Father does appear, his commitment to Nazi ideology is clear. He defends his work, claiming 'we are correcting history here' (p.148), and believes it is evidence that he is 'a patriot'. Furthermore, he perpetuates the anti-Semitism of the Nazis, telling Bruno that the people on the other side of the fence are 'not people at all' and that he has 'nothing whatsoever in common with them' (p.55).

Boyne counters Father's anti-Semitic rejection of Jewish humanity by accentuating the shared humanity of Bruno and Shmuel, and the kindness of Pavel, so that the reader is positioned to repudiate any of the falsities that come from Father's mouth. Father expects silent obedience from everyone around him, including his children, and even his wife; he clings to patriarchal notions that a man's word is final, telling his wife, when she dares express an opinion, 'I don't want to hear another word on the subject' (p.128). While some might consider Father's loss of the will to live in the final lines of the book to indicate his redemption, his continued commitment to the Final Solution after Bruno's disappearance cannot be ignored.

Mother

Key quotes

'War is not a fit subject for conversation.' (Mother, p.71)
'It's horrible … Just horrible. I can't stand it any more.' (Mother, p.193)

Mother is another family member who suffers collateral damage from Father's dedication to his 'important job' (p.5). In front of the children, Mother defends Father's work, fulfilling the patriarchal expectations of a dutiful wife, yet over time she becomes increasingly depressed and disgusted with what her husband is doing, disdainfully asking her husband, 'You call this work?' and declaring, 'I can't stand it any more' (p.193). Unfortunately, Mother's adherence to playing the role of dutiful wife by not speaking against her husband in front of the children (other than with passive-aggressive allusions to 'some people', p.9) contributes to Bruno's continued ignorance and thus his tragic death.

Mother is described by Bruno as 'a great believer in not playing favourites' (p.5) and on several occasions proves herself to be a fair and compassionate person. Firstly, she defends Herr Roller against Bruno's accusation that he is 'crazy' (p.70), explaining that 'he suffered a terrible injury during the Great War' (p.70), and telling Bruno that he has 'no idea of what the young men went through back then' (p.71). She again shows compassion by concealing that Pavel had helped Bruno with his injuries from the swing, saying, 'If the Commandant asks, we'll say that I cleaned Bruno up' (p.88). While Bruno thinks this act is 'terribly selfish' (p.88), in reality she is preventing Pavel from receiving a terrible beating, or perhaps worse. However, the ongoing isolation and the emotional toll of life at Out-With sees her turn to her 'medicinal sherries' (p.172) and the company of Lieutenant Kotler.

Lieutenant Kotler

Key quotes

'[Kotler] looked … as if he had never seen a child before and wasn't quite sure what he was supposed to do with one: eat it, ignore it or kick it down the stairs.' (p.19)

'There was an atmosphere around [Kotler] that made Bruno feel very cold …' (p.73)

Nineteen-year-old Lieutenant Kotler is a German soldier who works for Bruno's father at Out-With. With his 'very blond hair' (p.19) and obvious anti-Semitic views, Kotler embodies the Aryan ideal that was promoted in Nazi ideology. Kotler's cruelty contrasts with Pavel and Bruno's innate kindness and humanity. Bruno seems to instinctively know what Kotler is capable of before he witnesses any of his many cruelties. Kotler taunts Bruno, calling him 'little man' (p.74), but his cruelty towards Jews is far worse. When he instructs Pavel to help Bruno construct his tyre swing, he calls him names and 'spat a little as he spoke' (p.78), in a prelude to the violence he exhibits when Pavel spills wine on him, beating the man in a way that is simply described as 'unexpected and extremely unpleasant' and something that 'none of them could watch' (p.153). Such actions, though shocking to the reader, even in their highly sanitised form, were typical of the actions of Nazi soldiers.

Despite Kotler's vehement adherence to Nazi ideology, his character also functions as evidence of how arbitrary and authoritarian Hitler's regime was. Kotler is transferred away from Out-With suddenly, never to be heard from again. While it is possible that it could be because of his implied affair with Mother, it is more likely a consequence of the dinner-time revelation that his father was a professor of literature who had moved to Switzerland in 1938, thus marking him as a 'traitor' (p.151). Kotler is nervous and panicky when Father finishes the subject in front of the children with the ominous instruction to Kotler, 'We can discuss it in more depth at a later time' (p.152).

Grandmother

Key quote

'That's all you soldiers are interested in anyway ... Looking handsome in your fine uniforms. Dressing up and doing the terrible, terrible things you do.' (p.96)

Bruno's grandmother and Father's mother, Nathalie is a woman who loves to sing and clearly loves her grandchildren, as conveyed by Bruno's fond recollections of her devising a play for herself and the children to perform every Christmas. What makes Grandmother so remarkable is her willingness to speak out – an unusual and enviable trait within the context of the novel. It is through her that the reader receives a brief indication that support for Hitler and the ideology of the Nazis was not universal. In contrast to Grandfather, who is 'very proud of his son' (p.93), Grandmother is 'unimpressed' (p.93), lamenting that she is to blame for dressing him up 'like a puppet on a string' (p.94) when he was a boy, thus implying that Father is now a puppet for Hitler. She labels the actions of the Nazis as 'terrible' and declares herself 'ashamed' (p.96). Perhaps as evidence of Grandmother's powerlessness to counter the Nazi propaganda machine, at her funeral Father disregards what he knows his mother felt by wearing his uniform and celebrating that a floral wreath was sent by Hitler.

THEMES, IDEAS & VALUES

The causes and consequences of ignorance

Key quotes

'It's so unfair ... I don't see why I have to be stuck over here ... and you get to have dozens of friends and are probably playing for hours every day.' (Bruno to Shmuel, p.114)

'"I'm asking you, if we're not Jews, what are we instead?"
"We're the opposite," said Gretel ...' (Bruno and Gretel, p.189)

At the beginning of Boyne's novel, Bruno is the personification of innocence; he has not yet been corrupted by the hatred perpetuated by the Nazis. He looks upon the events around him with incomprehension and therefore remains ignorant of the horrors and dangers that surround him. Boyne's most overt tool to convey this ignorance is the limited narrative viewpoint, which controls the reader's knowledge of events and captures Bruno's naive interpretation of what he sees.

Bruno's parents are particularly to blame for his (and initially Gretel's) ignorance. Perhaps to protect his innocence, Mother answers Bruno's questions with vague generalisations. For example, when he seeks to understand why they must move, Mother repeatedly states that Father has been given a job that is 'very special' (p.4) and 'very important' (p.5), yet not once does she explain what that job entails. Once they arrive at Out-With, Bruno and Gretel's incomprehension of what they see outside his window is clear. Gretel asks herself, 'Who are all those people?' (p.37), and Bruno asks the same question of Father in the subsequent chapter. While Father does not evade Bruno's questions in the same way as Mother, he responds with anti-Semitic rhetoric, declaring, 'Those people ... well, they're not people at all, Bruno' (p.55). Such rhetoric is also spouted by Herr Liszt, whose job it is teach Bruno 'about the great wrongs that have been done' to him (p.101), yet such lessons also fail to answer Bruno's fundamental question: why the people in the 'striped pyjamas' are kept on the other side of the fence. Bruno seeks answers from Maria, yet she instructs him to 'stay quiet and concentrate on [his] school work' (p.67), and Gretel simply declares that the people are 'Jews' who 'can't mix with us' (p.188).

The lack of meaningful answers to Bruno's questions from those in his own household leaves a void that he (and the reader) must therefore fill. Bruno's partial view from his window, where amorphous figures in striped pyjamas disappear from view, symbolises the gaps in his knowledge. The kindness he receives from Pavel (and Pavel's incongruous revelation that he was once a doctor) prompts Bruno to ask further questions in the hope of filling this void, while his meeting and friendship with Shmuel give him another source to develop his understanding.

Unfortunately, even with Shmuel sitting before him and explaining the reality of his experiences, Bruno is either unable or unwilling to shatter his own ignorance. There are some questions that Bruno simply will not ask because the answers will force him to confront the reality of what Father is overseeing. For example, when Shmuel recounts his horrific tale of first being confined to the ghetto in Cracow and then being transported to Out-With, Bruno naively reflects that 'it didn't seem like such a terrible thing to him, and after all much the same thing had happened to him' (p.134). Such wilful blindness is also evident when Shmuel declares, 'There aren't any good soldiers' (p.144). Rather than ask his friend to elaborate on this, Bruno counters with, 'Except Father', because 'Father was Father, and Bruno didn't think it was right for someone to say something bad about him' (p.144). Such instances where Bruno chooses not to see what is right in front of him indicate that sometimes ignorance is a state that we choose for ourselves, because the truth may shatter the secure foundations of our sheltered existence.

Boyne's novel has been criticised for imbuing Bruno with a degree of innocence that many consider unrealistic for the time. Boyne defends this, arguing that Bruno's innocence and ignorance are crucial to the story because they imply a wider question: 'how could so many millions of people have been murdered under the eyes of the whole world without anyone knowing about it?' (bookreporter 2006). Just as Bruno's innocence and ignorance are key reasons that he ultimately wanders into his death, the blindness of the world to the plight of Jews during the Holocaust similarly caused the tragic deaths of millions.

Violence and trauma

Key quote

'"You don't know what it's like here," said Shmuel eventually in a low voice, his words barely carrying across to Bruno.
"You don't have any sisters, do you?" asked Bruno quickly, pretending he hadn't heard that because then he wouldn't have to answer.' (pp.144–5)

A brutal reality of the Holocaust is that horrific and unimaginable acts of violence were perpetrated, especially against Jewish people. As *The Boy in the Striped Pyjamas* looks through Bruno's ignorant eyes at the world around him, the reader is spared detailed accounts of what was done by German soldiers. There are several instances in the narrative where there is clear and unavoidable evidence of inhumane acts of violence, yet Bruno seems to avoid directing his gaze at these moments, which are only given fleeting attention, such as when Lieutenant Kotler beats Pavel. It could be argued that this act of avoidance by Bruno is not evidence of ignorance of what is going on, but a traumatic response where he seeks to evade the emotional pain generated by witnessing Nazi brutality.

When Bruno looks through his bedroom window (first by himself and then with Gretel), there are some distinct clues that it is a disturbing sight. The view makes him 'feel very cold and unsafe' (p.21), and he stands open-mouthed at what he sees. This imagery implies that the sight before him is both shocking and distressing, an idea confirmed by the children's consensus that it is a 'nasty-looking place' (p.34). It is also clearly a sight for which the children do not have a frame of reference: Gretel determines that it 'must be the countryside' (p.34) but Bruno rejects this theory, focusing on the traumatic image of children 'being shouted at' and 'crying' (p.38). Yet, significantly, Bruno 'turn[s] away' (p.40) after making his observations and seems to block these memories when he subsequently meets Shmuel. Even though Shmuel clearly articulates how difficult life is for him on his side of the fence, Bruno continues to imagine that it is unfair: 'you get to have dozens of friends and are probably playing for hours every day' (p.114). It is only when Bruno crawls under the fence that the fantasy he has constructed of life on the other side is shattered. Through Bruno's responses, Boyne is able to enhance the reader's understanding of why some people turned a blind eye to horrific acts (such as those witnessed by many during the Holocaust) – because the act of seeing requires a level of bravery and strength that not everyone possesses.

Nationalism and the justification of violence

Key quotes

'Well, because Germany is the greatest of all countries.' (Bruno, p.115)
'We are correcting history here.' (Father, p.148)

Throughout the narrative, Boyne provides insights into how nationalist rhetoric can be used by regimes to justify acts of persecution and violence. As the son of a Nazi Commandant, Bruno provides a point of view rarely encountered in Holocaust literature: placing the reader in the position of listening with the same wide-eyed astonishment as Bruno to the nationalist pride expressed by many of the authority figures surrounding him. When Bruno and Gretel meet the Fury, they get a glimpse of the ideas that drive the German leader. Gretel's proud boast that she can speak French is met with disgust and disdain by the Fury, who responds, 'Yes, but why would you want to?' (p.125). This moment gives the reader a brief glimpse of the rhetoric that dominated Hitler's speeches, in which he emphasised German superiority and invoked a sense of pride in German national identity.

The effectiveness of such language is shown on numerous occasions by Herr Liszt, Father, Grandfather, and even Bruno. Herr Liszt tells Bruno that he must learn of the 'great wrongs' Germany has suffered (p.101), foreshadowing Father's insistence that they 'are correcting history here' (p.148). Grandfather echoes these sentiments, telling Father that he is proud to see his son helping Germany 'reclaim her pride after all the great wrongs that were done to her' (p.95). Each of these comments, which refer to the harsh conditions imposed on Germany in the Treaty of Versailles, are repetitions of the recurring theme of Hitler's speeches and of Nazi propaganda in general. The effectiveness of such propaganda is evident when Bruno first meets Shmuel. In contrast to Shmuel, who can speak multiple languages and better understands the geography of Europe, Bruno is almost embarrassingly ignorant. Not knowing where Poland is, Bruno calls upon 'something that he had overheard Father discussing with Grandfather on any number of occasions' and boasts that 'Germany is the greatest of all countries', saying, 'We're superior' (p.115). Bruno's unthinking absorption of the ideology that was used to justify the persecution of Jews and other minorities demonstrates the ease with which people such as Hitler could gain control over large cohorts of people.

The suffering caused by prejudice

Key quotes

'Those people ... well, they're not people at all, Bruno.' (Father, p.55)

'Bruno couldn't help but notice that [Shmuel's hand] was like the hand of the pretend skeleton that Herr Liszt had brought with him one day when they were studying human anatomy.' (p.172)

Fences, walls, clothing and symbols all serve as visible metaphors of the physical and social boundaries imposed by the Nazis to separate Jewish people from the rest of the population of German-occupied Europe. A central strategy employed in Nazi propaganda was to create an image of Jewish otherness. The message of this propaganda is most clearly encapsulated in the attitudes of Father and, later, Gretel. Father instructs Bruno that the Jews are 'not people at all' and that he has 'nothing whatsoever in common with them' (p.55), while Gretel later tells Bruno that the fence is important for ensuring the Jews are 'with their own kind' because 'they can't mix with us' (p.188). Such language was one way of establishing a boundary between Jews and 'the Opposite' (p.189). Clothing served as another strategy. The camp clothing which consisted of 'a pair of grey striped pyjamas with a grey striped cap' (p.40) is the most obvious of these, but in their conversations Bruno and Shmuel also reveal that armbands served a similar function of marking Jews as separate, with the Jewish star serving as a means of identification that starkly contrasted with the Nazi armband worn by people like Father.

Such markers of supposed difference became the tools which helped the Nazis to justify their cruel treatment of the Jews. Shmuel's recount of his experience of being made to move to a ghetto in 'a different part of Cracow, where the soldiers built a big wall' (p.131), before arriving in Out-With where 'Mama was taken away' (p.133), provides a glimpse of the suffering of millions of Jewish people because of Nazi prejudice and persecution. This takes an even more harrowing turn when the reader sees the persecution writ large on Shmuel's body as he is starved to the point where his hand is 'like the hand of [a] pretend skeleton' (p.172). Through Bruno's perspective, Boyne challenges the reader to see how terribly inhumane and immoral the treatment of Jewish people was. Just as Shmuel transforms from 'a blob' to 'a figure' to 'a boy' (p.108), the millions of Jewish victims of the Holocaust become individuals, each with their own life story, for whom readers are positioned to feel great compassion and sorrow.

Fear and silence

Key quote

'Bruno, if you have any sense at all, you will stay quiet ... We must all just keep ourselves safe until this is all over ... What more can we do than that after all? It's not up to us to change things.' (Maria, p.67)

While Boyne clearly condemns characters such as Father and Lieutenant Kotler, who are directly responsible for perpetrating violence against Jewish people, he also draws attention to the culpability of those who maintain their silence in the face of wrongdoing.

Through clues embedded within the narrative, Boyne makes it clear that both Mother and Maria are uncomfortable with what is happening at Out-With, but are either unwilling or afraid to speak their minds. At the very least, Mother feels frustration with having to move to Out-With, telling Bruno, 'We don't have a choice in this' (p.8) and 'We don't have the luxury of thinking' (p.15). Such comments indicate that Mother has abdicated responsibility for speaking against what is being done to her own family, let alone what is being done to the Jews. This is perhaps a consequence of her subservience to Father in their patriarchal household, although Grandmother's willingness to speak out against her son's role implies some cowardice on Mother's part. Similarly, Maria believes that her subservient role as a maid in the household renders her incapable of using her voice. She perpetually walks through the household with her eyes averted, avoiding engaging with the Nazi soldiers, including Father, because, she says, 'it's not up to us to change things' (p.67). The women's refusal to speak out is most clear when Pavel is beaten by Kotler and nobody 'stepped in to stop him ... even though none of them could watch' (p.153).

Bruno clearly absorbs these lessons, leading him to conclude that 'he would do well to keep his mouth shut' (p.153). Boyne highlights the danger of such an attitude, which exposes those who are most in need of protection. This is no more apparent than when Bruno fails to defend Shmuel in front of Lieutenant Kotler – he does not speak out because he feels 'just as terrified himself' (p.177) and, as a consequence, Shmuel suffers a terrible beating at the hands of a man whom the reader knows is capable of great violence.

Boyne suggests that, by turning a blind eye to the atrocities being committed at their doorstep (and indeed in their home), these characters create a space in which the Nazis are endowed with an even greater sense that what they are doing is right. The lack of dissenting voices (other than that of Grandmother) helps to perpetuate the idea that the inhumane crimes can continue uninhibited. Silence, Boyne warns, can be just as harmful as prejudice.

Loneliness

Key quotes

'[H]e no longer had any friends to play with, and it wasn't as if Gretel would ever play with him.' (p.102)

'There was no one for her to talk to, and the only person who she had been remotely friendly with – the young Lieutenant Kotler – had been transferred somewhere else.' (Bruno about Mother, p.192)

Several of the characters in *The Boy in the Striped Pyjamas* suffer from being lonely. For Bruno, Gretel and Mother, this is a consequence of being dislocated from the familiar environment of Berlin to Out-With. In their new home, they lack the bonds with others that are needed to feel a sense of ease, and so each goes in search of ways to soothe their loneliness.

Boyne contrasts the life and busyness of Berlin, where 'there were always people strolling along and stopping to chat' (p.13), with the emptiness and desolation of Out-With, which is in the 'middle of nowhere' and 'cold' (p.14). Such imagery accentuates the isolation and loneliness that is subsequently felt. Bruno's key concern when he is told that they are leaving Berlin is that he must 'say goodbye' (p.7) to his 'three best friends for life' (p.8). Bruno is desperate for companionship, seeking out conversation with Gretel even though he thinks she is a 'Hopeless

Case' (p.3), and Maria, even though 'talking to a maid wasn't quite the same thing as having some friends to talk to' (p.58). Gretel similarly finds herself lonely because 'back in Berlin she had had Hilda and Isobel and Louise to play with' but in Out-With she 'had no one at all except her collection of lifeless dolls' (p.160), while Mother becomes increasingly withdrawn and notably absent as Bruno's narrative progresses.

To cope, these characters search for solutions to their loneliness. Bruno's loneliness manifests as rule-breaking in the form of exploration, and thus he finds a solution to his solitude in his chance encounter with Shmuel. When Bruno meets Shmuel he feels 'very happy all of a sudden' because he believes he has found a friend and he realises 'how lonely he had been at Out-With' (p.113). Gretel also seeks companionship, but, without any peers around for her to bond with, she seeks connection with Lieutenant Kotler, forming a crush on him that is evident in her use of a 'silly voice' (p.75) when around the young soldier. Gretel also channels her time into absorbing the lessons of Herr Liszt. Boyne implies that her pride in being German gives Gretel a sense of belonging that she is unable to obtain elsewhere, thus highlighting one of the key tools of recruitment often used by groups who may have radical views but provide an avenue of escape from the torment of social isolation. Mother also seeks companionship with Lieutenant Kotler, and it is implied that she forms an adulterous relationship with him. However, when Kotler is 'transferred somewhere else' (p.192) she becomes 'very quiet' and spends much of her time sleeping or indulging in 'medicinal sherries' (p.194). Through these characters, Boyne conveys the damage that can be caused by loneliness and isolation, thus emphasising the importance of human connection and a sense of belonging.

Friendship

Key quotes

'Shmuel, I'm ashamed of myself.' (Bruno, p.181)
'You're my best friend, Shmuel … My best friend for life.' (Bruno, p.220)

Boyne reveals the power of friendship in his novel through the powerful bond that develops over time between Bruno and Shmuel. The deep connection shared by the boys is symbolically expressed through the mirroring that occurs. The boys sit down on the ground on opposite sides of the fence, each with legs crossed like the other, and quickly learn that they were 'born on the same day' (p.113).

For both Bruno and Shmuel, the companionship they offer one another serves as a counterpoint to their loneliness. During their first meeting Bruno feels 'very happy all of a sudden' (p.113) that he has found Shmuel. Desperate to find someone with whom he has something in common, Bruno initially seems oblivious to what his new friend is going through: when Shmuel recalls the experience of being relocated to Out-With, Bruno shouts, 'That happened to me too!' (p.131). For Shmuel, the daily conversations provide a brief respite from the horrors to which he is subjected, and, at a more prosaic level, a potential avenue to get some desperately needed food. Bruno is perceptive enough to note 'just how small and skinny his new friend was' (p.136), and, over time, he comes to realise how much his friend is suffering; when he tells Gretel some of Shmuel's stories he finally realises 'how sad that must have made his friend' and feels a responsibility 'to say anything to cheer Shmuel up' (p.163). Through their conversations, Bruno is exposed to new ideas and develops a limited ability to look beyond his own selfish needs and to care for the wellbeing of a fellow human being. While the friendship is tested during the incident when Bruno fails to defend Shmuel against Kotler, the bond between the boys becomes stronger. Boyne conveys this through the highly symbolic moment when, after Bruno apologises for letting his friend down, Shmuel 'lifted the bottom of the fence up ... reached his hand out ... and then the two boys shook hands and smiled at each other' (p.181). This moment of amity signifies the power of friendship to overcome barriers, whether they be physical (like the fence) or social constructs (such as prejudice). Even in the horrifying final moments of the boys' lives, they prove that friendship can endure in times of darkness, as they continue to hold hands 'despite the chaos that followed' (p.220).

DIFFERENT INTERPRETATIONS

Different interpretations arise from different responses to a text. Over time, a text will evoke a wide range of responses from its readers, who may come from various social or cultural groups and live in very different places and historical periods. Responses by critics and reviewers can be published in newspapers, journals and books, both online and in print. They can also be expressed in discussions among readers in the media, classrooms, book groups and so on.

While there is no single correct reading or interpretation of a text, it is important to understand that an interpretation is more than a personal opinion – it is the justification of a point of view on the text. To present an interpretation of a text based on your point of view, you must use a logical argument and support it with relevant evidence from the text.

Critical viewpoints

The Boy in the Striped Pyjamas has divided scholars and critics. While many feel that Boyne cleverly and effectively conveys the horrors of the Holocaust in a format that enables young readers to be educated on the topic, others have expressed concern that the novel diminishes the historical realities of the Holocaust. As the novel has been an enormous publishing success and is part of the syllabus in many schools, it continues to draw much critical attention.

One of the key reasons the text is celebrated and taught is its ability to present a complex and traumatic aspect of our history in a form that is accessible to children. In her review for *The Guardian*, Kathryn Hughes (2006) argues that the power of the text lies in 'the slow revelation of detail' that 'becomes an education in real time of the horrors of "Out-With"' and that Bruno's innocence is representative of the 'wilful refusal of all adult Germans to see what was going on under their noses' during the Holocaust. In her detailed analysis of the use of Bruno's naive narrative viewpoint, Alice Curry (2010) similarly argues for the effectiveness of Boyne's approach. She contends that Bruno's narrative viewpoint draws the reader's attention to the 'blind spaces' in the narrative (the spaces that are occupied by the marginalised Jews) in a way that condemns 'cultural ignorance and political apathy' and advocates 'multicultural awareness' (p.71). In other words, the text effectively directs the reader to mimic Bruno by asking questions about what is going on in the margins. San José Rico and Fernández (2011) echo this argument, asserting that the power of the text is its ability to give 'voice to such atrocities' and prevent forgetting, and that it pays 'homage to all those victims by giving voice to their suffering and bringing to the public eye the knowledge of the atrocities so that, hopefully, they will never be repeated' (p.314).

The naive narrative voice is seen by some as a critical flaw within the novel. Pettitt (2014) believes that the reconfiguration and reduction of the Holocaust to an accessible and palatable narrative is problematic, because it relies on the reader being able to fill the 'epistemic gaps' (p.160) that are created by Bruno's ignorance. Pettitt argues, 'since texts that are aimed at children function primarily by means of obscuring the history of the Holocaust, the question as to how a particularly young or uninformed child reader is to comprehend the didactic message' (p.162) is a glaring flaw. Without the guidance and support of an informed adult, the child reader is unable to experience the full shocking effect of the denouement because 'any indication of suffering, misery and violence remains obscured' (p.160). Matthews (2014) concurs with this assertion, but also expresses concern that 'historical inaccuracies are chosen to serve the plot and ... raise many concerns about the ethics of dealing with the Holocaust in fiction' (p.78).

Furthermore, a core problem identified in many criticisms of the text is that the reader is ultimately positioned to sympathise with the wrong people. Randall (2019) criticises the fact that 'the reader's attention remains with the experience of the concentration camp commandant and his wife whose son had been killed'. Similarly, Lassner and Cohen (2014) accuse Boyne of misdirecting audience sympathies 'away from the Jewish victims of the gas chambers and onto the Nazi family' (p.170). In other words, it is ultimately the tragedy of the death of a single fictional boy that the reader is moved by, rather than the actual deaths of millions of Jewish victims of the Holocaust.

Two interpretations

Interpretation 1: In *The Boy in the Striped Pyjamas*, John Boyne reveals the very worst of humanity.

John Boyne's novel presents humanity's capacity to behave in truly loathsome ways. Through the actions of his characters, it becomes clear that some people are capable of shocking acts of violence, while others are willing to turn a blind eye to injustice.

The glimpses of the horrific treatment of Jewish people in 'Out-With' in Boyne's novel hint at the actions of the Nazis in Auschwitz and other Nazi death camps. For example, when Bruno looks through his window he witnesses people 'trying to keep their heads up' (p.37) and 'a group of children … being shouted at by a group of soldiers' (p.38). This cruelty is brought into sharper focus through the actions of Lieutenant Kotler, who at various stages beats Pavel and Shmuel and even intimidates Bruno. Kotler reminds Bruno of 'the big boys at school, the ones he always steered clear of' (p.74), yet Bruno fails to recognise that his father is also like those boys, as indicated when Shmuel wonders 'how such a man could have a son who was so friendly and kind' (p.202). Almost as shocking as the violence of the Nazis is the ideology they use to justify these acts. Father believes that the actions he is overseeing at Out-With are justified because Jewish people are 'not people at all' (p.55). He dehumanises the Jewish prisoners by shaving their heads and forcing them all to wear the same 'striped pyjamas'. Such actions are justified with the argument that 'we are correcting history here' (p.148), and are embraced by other Germans, as shown through Gretel, who tells her brother that Jews 'can't mix with us' (p.188).

The novel also confronts the reader with the reality that, even in the face of great injustice, most people are willing to stand aside and 'accept the situation' (pp.55–6) in which they find themselves. Maria clearly lives by the advice she gives to Bruno, which is to 'stay quiet' and keep himself safe because, she says, 'It's not up to us to change things' (p.67). Similarly, Mother clearly feels some degree of compassion, shown when she conceals the fact that Pavel helped Bruno, in order to protect the elderly Jewish man; however, she fails to speak out against what her husband is doing, instead allowing her children to be tutored by Herr Liszt so that they too will share in the damaging ideology of the Nazis. Most distressingly, Bruno shows that even friendship is sometimes not enough to drive an individual to stand up for what is right. When Shmuel tries to defend himself against Lieutenant Kotler by telling him that Bruno gave him some chicken because the boys are friends, Bruno denies knowing Shmuel, declaring, 'I've never seen him before in my life' (p.178).

The cowardice and cruelty exhibited by the characters in *The Boy in the Striped Pyjamas* prove that there is no end to the depths of human depravity.

Interpretation 2: Despite its bleak ending, *The Boy in the Striped Pyjamas* celebrates the human capacity for kindness.

Although *The Boy in the Striped Pyjamas* is set during one of the darkest periods of human history, it still manages to portray and celebrate the kindness and compassion that people are capable of, even when they have had everything taken from them.

Generous acts of kindness are witnessed throughout Boyne's novel. When Bruno falls from his tyre swing and is injured, Pavel comes to his aid even though he puts himself at risk of violent retribution from the Nazi soldiers for daring to speak to the Commandant's son. Bruno instinctively responds to Pavel's 'quiet voice' (p.81) and immediately feels safe as Pavel tends to his wounds, and when Bruno shows signs of panic Pavel calms him by assuring him, 'I certainly am a doctor' (p.85). This is a dangerous revelation for Pavel that would likely see him killed immediately if it was discovered, yet he says it because it is what his patient needs. Mother repays this act of kindness by providing Pavel with protection from retribution, promising to tell Father, 'I cleaned Bruno up' if he asks (p.88). These small moments prove that self-interest is not an impediment to doing the right thing.

Through the friendship of Bruno and Shmuel, Boyne also reveals that strong emotional bonds can elicit courage and kindness. Although Bruno sometimes allows his self-interest to override his loyalty to Shmuel, such as when he fails to defend Shmuel against Kotler, he ultimately proves the depths of his affection by helping Shmuel to look for his father in Out-With. Even though Bruno quickly realises, 'I don't think I like it here' (p.215), he stays true to his promise and continues the search. Bruno's gesture of taking 'Shmuel's tiny hand in his and squeez[ing] it tightly' and telling him he is his 'best friend for life' (p.220) as the terrified boys are crowded into the gas chamber is proof of Bruno's enduring humanity.

While moments of genuine selflessness are not common in *The Boy in the Striped Pyjamas*, the moments of kindness witnessed are so poignant that they stand against the darkest and most depressing moments in the novel and remind us of the very best that humanity has to offer.

QUESTIONS & ANSWERS

This section focuses on your own analytical writing on the text, and gives you strategies for producing high-quality responses in your coursework and exam essays.

Essay writing – an overview

An essay on a literary work is a formal and serious piece of writing that presents your point of view on the text, usually in response to a given topic. Your 'point of view' in an essay is your interpretation of the meaning of the text's language, structure, characters, situations and events, supported by detailed analysis of textual evidence.

Analyse – don't summarise

In your essays it is important to avoid simply summarising what happens in a text.

- A **summary** is a description or paraphrase (retelling in different words) of the characters and events. For example: 'Macbeth has a horrifying vision of a dagger dripping with blood before he goes to murder King Duncan.'
- An **analysis** is an explanation of the real meaning or significance that lies 'beneath' the text's words (and images, for a film). For example: 'Macbeth's vision of a bloody dagger shows how deeply uneasy he is about the violent act he is contemplating, and conveys his sense that supernatural forces are impelling him to act.'

A limited amount of summary is sometimes necessary to let your reader know which part of the text you wish to discuss. However, always keep this to a minimum and follow it immediately with your analysis of what this part of the text is really telling us.

Plan your essay

Carefully plan your essay so that you have a clear idea of what you are going to say. The plan ensures that your ideas flow logically, that your argument remains consistent and that you stay on the topic. An essay plan should be a list of **brief dot points** covering no more than half a page.

- Include your central argument or main contention – a concise statement of your overall response to the topic.
- Write three or four dot points for each paragraph, indicating the main idea and evidence/examples from the text. Note that in your essay you will need to *expand* on these points and analyse the evidence.

Structure your essay

An essay is a complete, self-contained piece of writing. It has a clear beginning (the introduction), middle (several body paragraphs) and end (the last paragraph or conclusion). It must also have a central argument that runs throughout, linking each paragraph to form a coherent whole. See examples of introductions and conclusions in the 'Analysing a sample topic' and 'Sample answer' sections.

The introduction establishes your overall response to the topic. It includes your main contention and outlines the main evidence you will refer to in the course of the essay. Write your introduction *after* you have done a plan and *before* you write the rest of the essay.

The body paragraphs argue your case – they present evidence from the text and explain how this evidence supports your argument. Each body paragraph needs:

- a strong **topic sentence** (usually the first sentence) that states the main point being made in the paragraph
- **evidence** from the text, including some brief quotations

- **analysis** of the textual evidence, with **explanation** of its significance and how it supports your argument
- **links back to the topic** in one or more statements, usually towards the end of the paragraph.

Connect the body paragraphs so that your discussion flows smoothly. Use some linking words and phrases such as 'similarly' and 'on the other hand', though don't start every paragraph like this. Another strategy is to use a significant word from the last sentence of one paragraph in the first sentence of the next.

Use key terms from the topic – or synonyms for them – throughout, so the relevance of your discussion to the topic is always clear.

The conclusion ties everything together and finishes the essay. It includes strong statements that emphasise your central argument and provide a clear response to the topic.

Avoid simply restating the points made earlier in the essay – this will end on a very flat note and imply that you have run out of ideas and vocabulary. The conclusion should be a logical extension of what you have written, not just a repetition or summary of it. Writing an effective conclusion can be a challenge. Try using these tips:

- Start by linking back to the final sentence of the second-last paragraph, rather than leaping to your main contention straight away – this helps your writing to flow.
- Use synonyms and expressions with equivalent meanings to vary your vocabulary. This allows you to reinforce your line of argument without being repetitive.
- When planning your essay, think of one or two broad statements or observations about the text's wider meaning. These should be related to the topic and your overall argument. Keep them for the conclusion, since they will give you something 'new' to say but still follow logically from your discussion. The introduction will be focused on the topic, but the conclusion can present a wider view of the text.

Essay topics

1 'In *The Boy in the Striped Pyjamas*, characters are overwhelmingly selfish and self-serving.' To what extent do you agree?

2 'The parents in *The Boy in the Striped Pyjamas* deserve our sympathy, not our condemnation.' Discuss.

3 'The characters in *The Boy in the Striped Pyjamas* are motivated more by fear than by anything else.' Do you agree?

4 To what extent do Bruno and Shmuel demonstrate that friendship can overcome barriers?

5 "[I]f that was the kind of thing that went on at Out-With then he'd better not disagree with anyone any more about anything; in fact he would do well to keep his mouth shut ..."
How does Boyne emphasise the danger of remaining silent?

6 "It was almost (Shmuel thought) as if they were all exactly the same really."
How does Boyne emphasise the humanity of the Jewish prisoners in his novel?

7 'It is easier to be brave when you are ignorant of the dangers you are facing.' Discuss.

8 'Bruno is an inherently selfish boy.' To what extent do you agree?

9 'Power is a corrupting and dangerous force.'
Consider how Boyne conveys this idea in his novel.

10 'By hiding the atrocities of the Holocaust from his readers, Boyne dishonours the memories of all those who died.' Do you agree?

Vocabulary for writing on *The Boy in the Striped Pyjamas*

Anti-Semitism: hatred of or prejudice against Jewish people.

Denouement: the end of a book or a play, where everything is resolved/ explained.

Final Solution: a plan made by the Nazis during World War II to kill all the Jews in Europe.

Holocaust: the systematic state-sponsored killing of six million Jewish people during World War II.

Marginalised: treated as insignificant or unwanted – pushed to the sides.

Motif: an idea, image or pattern that is repeated.

Naive: lacking experience of life – a naive person tends to trust others or believe things too easily.

Narrative voice: the perspective/voice of the person telling the story.

Persecution: extremely bad treatment of someone, especially because of their race, religion or political beliefs.

Symbol: something or someone that represents a particular idea or quality.

Analysing a sample topic

"It was almost (Shmuel thought) as if they were all exactly the same really."

How does Boyne emphasise the humanity of the Jewish prisoners in his novel?

Before writing your response, assess the meaning of the key words in the topic. This topic focuses on the idea of 'humanity', which relates to the state of being human, and of behaving and thinking humanely (kindly and compassionately).

Whenever you are presented with a quote, take time to analyse and contextualise it: who said it, when and why? This quote occurs in a brief moment where the narrative shifts to Shmuel's viewpoint just after Bruno has put on the striped pyjamas and cap in preparation to crawl under the fence for their adventure. It accentuates how similar the two boys are.

The task word 'how' leads you to discuss the *ways* in which Boyne has constructed his novel to achieve his purpose, which is to emphasise the humanity of the Jewish prisoners. In organising your paragraphs, you should think about what some of those ways are, making use of the quote to inform one of your ideas. The following essay outline focuses on three key elements used by Boyne:

- the doubling/mirroring of Bruno and Shmuel to point out how much they have in common
- the characterisation of Pavel as a kind man, and the revelations of Pavel's and Shmuel's backgrounds
- the representation of the inhumane actions of Lieutenant Kotler and Father as a contrast to the kindness of Pavel.

Sample introduction

> A key strategy utilised by the Nazis to justify the systematic eradication of the Jewish population of Europe was to dehumanise Jewish people. In his fable *The Boy in the Striped Pyjamas*, John Boyne emphasises the humanity of Jewish people in an effort to break down the prejudicial ideas that were used to justify the Holocaust. By revealing the truth of Pavel and Shmuel's lives before they arrived at Out-With, and conveying their emotional depth, Boyne imbues these characters with humanity. Furthermore, Boyne presents the inhumane actions of the Nazi soldiers as a counterpoint to amplify the kindness of Pavel. Most importantly, the mirroring of Bruno and Shmuel, and the strong friendship the young boys forge, emphasises the idea that constructs such as race are artificial barriers that ignore the fact that we are all, ultimately, human.

Body paragraph outline

Paragraph 1: Through the characterisation of Pavel and Shmuel, Boyne ensures that the reader understands that these characters possess the most important human qualities of all: kindness and compassion.

- '"You were going too high," said Pavel in a quiet voice that immediately made Bruno feel safe.' (p.81)
- '"It's not that bad," said Pavel, but in a gentle and kindly voice.' (p.83)
- '"Young man," said Pavel … "I certainly am a doctor. Just because a man glances up at the sky at night does not make him an astronomer, you know."' (p.85)
- 'Before we came here I lived with my mother and father and my brother Josef … Every morning we ate our breakfast together at seven o'clock …' (p.129)
- When Bruno apologises to Shmuel: 'the two boys shook hands and smiled at each other'. (p.181)

Paragraph 2: The cruelty and prejudice of the Nazi soldiers stands in stark contrast to the gentle nature of the Jewish characters.

- 'He looked … as if he had never seen a child before and wasn't quite sure what he was supposed to do with one: eat it, ignore it or kick it down the stairs.' (p.19)
- 'There was an atmosphere around him that made Bruno feel very cold …' (p.73)
- 'What happened then was both unexpected and extremely unpleasant. Lieutenant Kotler grew very angry with Pavel and no one – not Bruno, not Gretel, not Mother and not even Father – stepped in to stop him doing what he did next, even though none of them could watch. Even though it made Bruno cry and Gretel grow pale.' (p.153)
- 'Do you think that I would have made such a success of my life if I hadn't learned when to argue and when to keep my mouth shut and follow orders? Well, Bruno? Do you?' (Father, p.52)

➔

- 'Shmuel bit his lip and said nothing. He had seen Bruno's father on any number of occasions and couldn't understand how such a man could have a son who was so friendly and kind.' (p.202)

Paragraph 3: It is ultimately the strong bond forged between Bruno and Shmuel that challenges any notion of difference between Jewish people and the rest of humanity.

- '"We're like twins," said Bruno. "A little bit," agreed Shmuel.' (p.113)
- '"I look just like you now," said Bruno sadly, as if this was a terrible thing to admit. "Only fatter," admitted Shmuel.' (p.191)
- 'It was almost (Shmuel thought) as if they were all exactly the same really.' (p.211)
- 'Bruno found that he was still holding Shmuel's hand in his own and nothing in the world would have persuaded him to let it go.' (p.220)

Sample conclusion

Through the innocent eyes of Bruno, John Boyne ultimately reveals that prejudice and persecution marginalised Jewish people. Yet Boyne conveys that, while the Nazis sought to dehumanise Jewish people by taking away their identities and their lives, they only managed to prove themselves to be inhumane. As proven by Bruno and Shmuel, when we remove the artificial barriers such as prejudice, we are 'all exactly the same really'.

SAMPLE ANSWER

'The parents in *The Boy in the Striped Pyjamas* deserve our sympathy, not our condemnation.' Discuss.

The power of John Boyne's fable *The Boy in the Striped Pyjamas* comes from the novel's distressing conclusion that witnesses the death of young German boy Bruno and his Jewish 'twin' Shmuel. This tragic outcome can drive the reader to feel sympathy for Bruno's parents for the loss of their son. Like Bruno, Mother has little choice in the move to 'Out-With', and she appears to be another victim of the autocratic Nazi regime. Yet it cannot be overlooked that neither parent bothers to ensure their son has an adequate understanding of the dangers that lie beyond the boundaries of their home. Furthermore, as the Commandant of the death camp, Father must be held directly responsible for the death of his own son, as well as of the millions of Jews whose murders he oversaw.

The lack of agency afforded to Mother suggests that she deserves some compassion from readers. From the moment Bruno discovers Maria packing all his belongings, it becomes apparent that Mother is uneasy about the move to 'Out-With'. Through the image of 'the rims of [Mother's] eyes [being] more red than usual', Boyne conveys Mother's distress at the announcement that they must move. The inclusion of herself when she informs Bruno, 'We don't have a choice in this' indicates that Mother, like Bruno, is in a position where she must simply accept that this is the will of 'the Fury' and Father. Bruno's subsequent recollection of his parents' overheard conversation after 'the Fury' came to dinner and informed Father of his new role furthers the reader's compassion for Mother. There is a suggestion that she does not agree with the Nazi treatment of Jews in the camp when she expresses distress that they must relocate to 'such a place', and this notion is reinforced by her deliberate act to protect Pavel from the repercussions of having dared to touch the Commandant's son by 'tak[ing] credit' for tending to Bruno's wounds after he falls off his swing. Such moments position the reader to view

Mother with compassion, seeing her as another victim of a society that stripped almost everybody of choice.

In failing to protect their son from the dangers that surround him in their new home, both parents deserve the condemnation of the reader. While Father's presence seems to loom over the entire text, he is notably absent from his son's life. Father remains inaccessible to Bruno, his office demarcated as 'Out Of Bounds At All Times And No Exceptions'. In the brief moments when Father deigns to speak to his son, he silences Bruno's questions, telling him that his success within the Nazi Party is a consequence of knowing 'when to keep [his] mouth shut and follow orders', thus denying Bruno the knowledge he needs to remain safe. Furthermore, while Mother does seem to have tenderness and affection for her son, the ongoing isolation and the emotional toll of living at 'Out-With' sees her turning to her 'medicinal sherries' and becoming almost as absent as Father. The failure of both Mother and Father to adequately parent their child makes them culpable in his death.

While some sympathy can be felt for Mother, Father deserves the reader's contempt. It is his adherence to the anti-Semitic ideas of the Nazi Party that creates the situation that allows his son to die. Father dehumanises the Jewish people, insisting that 'they're not people at all', and he firmly believes that what he is doing is 'important work' for both 'our country' and 'the Fury'. Like many German people, Father adheres to the idea that the Nazis 'are correcting history here', and for this reason he justifies the murder of millions in the gas chambers at the camp of which he is Commandant. Most damningly, Boyne provides a small clue as to how truly cruel Father is to the Jewish prisoners through the incredulous tone of Shmuel, who wonders 'how such a man could have a son who was so friendly and kind'. Father's own realisation that it was his actions, and his commands, that brought about his son's death is conveyed by the fact that, after this, 'he didn't really mind what [the Allied soldiers] did to him'. Father himself understands that he deserves no sympathy and must bear the burden of the knowledge of what his heinous acts brought about.

It is a natural response to feel compassion for anyone who suffers the death of a child. However, when the actions of Bruno's parents are examined, it becomes impossible to deny that they must be condemned for their abject failure to provide the safety and protection their son needed. As she has little control over her circumstances, some sympathy can be felt for Mother. Yet it is impossible to commiserate with Father, for he is the architect of his own misery and responsible for the deaths of a horrifying number of blameless people.

REFERENCES & READING

Text

Boyne, J 2012, *The Boy in the Striped Pyjamas*, Vintage, London. First published in 2006.

Newspaper articles

Boyne, J 2014, 'John Boyne: "The Catholic priesthood blighted my youth and the youth of people like me"', *The Irish Times*, 7 Nov, www.irishtimes.com/culture/books/john-boyne-the-catholic-priesthood-blighted-my-youth-and-the-youth-of-people-like-me-1.1991196

Clark, A 2021, 'John Boyne: "People were criticising my book when they hadn't read it"', *The Guardian*, 17 July, www.theguardian.com/books/2021/jul/17/john-boyne-people-were-criticising-my-book-when-they-hadnt-read-it

Books and journal articles

Curry, A 2010, 'The "Blind Space" that Lies Beyond the Frame', *International Research in Children's Literature*, vol. 3, no. 1, pp.61–74.

Hughes, K 2006, 'Educating Bruno', *The Guardian*, 21 Jan, https://www.theguardian.com/books/2006/jan/21/featuresreviews.guardianreview18

Hunter, A 2013, 'Tales from Over There: The Uses and Meanings of Fairy-Tales in Contemporary Holocaust Narrative', *Modernism/Modernity*, vol. 20, no. 1, pp.59–75.

Lassner, P and Cohen, D 2014, 'Magical transports and transformations: The lessons of children's holocaust fiction', *Studies in American Jewish Literature*, vol. 33, no. 2, pp.167–85.

Matthews, A 2014, *Navigating the Kingdom of Night*, University of Adelaide Press, pp.61–84.

Pettitt, J 2014, 'On Blends and Abstractions: Children's Literature and the Mechanisms of Holocaust Representation', *International Research in Children's Literature*, vol. 7, no. 2, pp.152–64.

Randall, H 2019, 'The Problem with "The Boy in The Striped Pyjamas"', *The Holocaust Exhibition and Learning Centre*, https://holocaustlearning.org.uk/latest/the-problem-with-the-boy-in-the-striped-pyjamas/

San José Rico, P and Fernández, M 2011, 'Escaping Trauma through a Dreamworld', *ES. Revista de Filología Inglesa*, vol. 32, pp.301–16.

Scott, A 2006, 'Something Is Happening', *New York Times Book Review*, 12 November, https://www.nytimes.com/2006/11/12/books/Scott.t.html

Websites

'Interview: September 15, 2006', Bookreporter.com, https://www.bookreporter.com/authors/john-boyne/news/interview-091406

'Treaty of Versailles', HISTORY, 2009, https://www.history.com/topics/world-war-i/treaty-of-versailles-1

United States Holocaust Memorial Museum, 'Introduction to the Holocaust', Holocaust Encyclopedia, https://encyclopedia.ushmm.org/content/en/article/introduction-to-the-holocaust